YouTube Influencer: The Ultimate Guide to YouTube Success, Content Creation, and Monetization Strategies

Build and Grow a Thriving YouTube Channel and Boost Engagement with Proven Techniques and Insider Secrets

Change Your Life Guru

Books by **Change Your Life Guru**:

Affiliate Marketing Mastery: *The Ultimate Guide to Starting Your Online Business and Earning Passive Income - Unlock Profitable Affiliate Secrets, Boost Earnings with Expert Strategies, Top Niches, High-Performance Products, Innovative Tactics and Essential Tools for Success*

Dropshipping Business Mastery: *The Ultimate Guide to Starting & Managing a Thriving Dropshipping Business - Skyrocket Your Income with Proven Strategies, Profitable Niches, and Unleash Powerful Marketing Tactics*

Etsy Store Mastery: *The Ultimate Guide to Building Your Own Etsy Empire - Learn Proven Strategies for Finding & Selling the Hottest Products, Building Your Brand, and Dominating Your Niche on Etsy*

Online Course Mastery: *The Ultimate Guide to Creating and Marketing Profitable Online Courses - Learn How to Find Your Niche, Create Engaging Content, and Succeed as an Online Course Creator*

Online Freelancing Mastery: *The Ultimate Guide to Making Money as an Online Freelancer - Unlock Proven Strategies to Monetize Your Skills and Talents, Market Yourself, and Go from Zero To Success*

Online Tutoring: *The Ultimate Guide to Creating a Profitable Online Tutoring Business — Become an Expert in Your Niche, Craft Engaging Sessions, Harness Powerful Marketing Strategies, and Profit from Your Expertise in the Digital Learning World*

Print on Demand Mastery: *The Ultimate Blueprint for Print on Demand Success - Unlock Actionable Tips & Strategies to Starting, Setting Up, and Marketing a Profitable Print on Demand Business*

Social Media Influencer: *The Ultimate Guide to Building a Profitable Social Media Influencer Career - Learn How to Build Your Brand, Create Viral Content, and Make Brands Beg to Pay for Your Lifestyle*

Subscription Business Model: *The Ultimate Guide to Building and Scaling A Predictable Recurring Income Business - Attract and Retain Loyal Subscribers, and Maximize Your Profitability with Proven Strategies and Best Practices*

YouTube Influencer: *The Ultimate Guide to YouTube Success, Content Creation, and Monetization Strategies - Build and Grow a Thriving YouTube Channel and Boost Engagement with Proven Techniques and Insider Secrets*

THANK YOU – A Gift For You!

THANK YOU for purchasing our book! *You could have chosen from dozens of other books on the same topic but you took a chance and chose this one.* As a token of our appreciation, we would like to offer you an exclusive **FREE GIFT BOX**. Your Gift Box contains powerful downloadable products, resources and tools that are the perfect companion to your newly-acquired book, and are designed to catapult you towards freedom and success.

To get instant access, just go to:
https://changeyourlife.guru/toolkit

Inside your Free Gift Box, you'll receive:

- **Goal Planners and Schedulers**: Map out manageable and actionable steps so you have clarity and are empowered with a clear roadmap to achieve every goal.

- **Expert Tips & Tricks:** Invaluable tips and strategies ready to apply to your life, or business, to accelerate your progress and reach your outcomes.

- **Exclusive Content:** Free bonus materials, resources, and tools to help you succeed.

- **New Freebies:** Enter your email address to download your free gift box and be updated when we add new Free Content, ensuring you always have the tools, information and strategies to sky-rocket your success!

Are you ready to supercharge your life? Download your gift box for FREE today! [**https://changeyourlife.guru/toolkit**]

Table of Contents

Introduction

Never give up on a dream just because of the time it will take to accomplish it. The time will pass anyway. –Earl Nightingale

Technology has been entwined in the way we live our lives. This became especially true when people were confined to their homes during the COVID-19 pandemic. We came to rely more than ever on our computers, smartphones, Wi-Fi, and TVs to keep us informed and entertained. And, of course, we cannot talk about technology or entertainment without making an honorable nod to YouTube.

Reports released in 2022 showed that YouTube is the second most used social media network globally. This isn't a surprise since the platform has approximately 2.1 billion active users around the globe. By starting your own YouTube channel, you can claim your share of such a great established audience and the associated earnings.

It's never too late to start your own YouTube channel, especially when considering that activity on the platform isn't showing any signs of slowing down. The opportunities are growing bigger and getting better. We can understand why some people may be reluctant to get started but if you're here, we assume that you'd like to take the first steps to get started!

Some believe that starting a YouTube channel is difficult. However, this book is the first step in the right direction and we will show you just how easy it is to start and run your own YouTube channel.

Creating content for your YouTube channel can seem daunting at first, considering your busy schedule if this is intended for a side hustle. However, creating videos crammed with content that you love and that makes you happy won't feel like work. While we cannot deny the fact that anything worth doing requires consistent effort, the responsibilities that come with running a YouTube channel are not as cumbersome as you may think. This book will ensure that you are equipped with all the information to start and run a successful YouTube channel.

If you are looking for a side hustle or a second stream of income, starting a YouTube channel is a great option! YouTube is also a great way to indulge in the hobbies and hidden passions you want to monetize. Many popular YouTubers have left their full-time jobs to pursue their dreams on YouTube.

Perhaps YouTube will always be a side hustle for you but who knows? Your YouTube channel might end up doing so well that you may have to do it full-time. You won't know whether you are cut out for it until you get started, and there is absolutely nothing to lose by giving it a try! Use this guide to turn your dreams into an actionable plan and create a success story you will live to cherish.

What's the Gain?

You may wonder, "Suppose I gather the confidence to start a YouTube channel, what's in it for me?" YouTube is a great source of passive income, not to mention a joyful hobby and a creative outlet that so many of us yearn for.

In 2020, YouTube generated revenues of about $19.7 billion and the platform is gaining more users daily. Here is a brief overview of the benefits of having your own YouTube channel:

- **It gives you access to a global audience:** With millions of people active on YouTube on a daily basis, YouTube accommodates an audience with varying characteristics in terms of age, gender, educational status, social background, and career paths, just to name a few. With such a diverse user base, you are bound to attract like-minded people to your channel by posting content that they are interested in.

- **It increases your online presence:** Have you ever searched for something on Google and the top result was a couple of YouTube videos? This is because of search engine optimization. Considering that YouTube is its own search engine, the opportunity of also appearing on Google searches provides a double advantage when it comes to your online presence.

- **Your channel gets streamlined traffic:** While there are many people actively looking for specific topics on YouTube, the algorithm will recommend your channel or videos to people who have searched for similar content to what you have created. For example, if you have a soap making video, a person who has searched "How to make soap" may get a recommendation to your video or channel based on the YouTube algorithm's suggestions.

- **It provides some level of connection with your audience:** Visual media is a great way to connect with your audience. For instance, when visiting a website, a visitor will read through the information but may lose interest if the content is complicated or technical. YouTube allows creators to visually present their ideas and products. Filming yourself using your products and portraying positive end results can also instill a level of trust in your viewers.

- **You are your own boss:** If you have always wanted to be your own boss, being a YouTuber is a great opportunity to give it a try. You plan your schedule and content to suit you. Your creativity can come into play without much interference.

This book has been carefully compiled to help you reach these benefits. We will provide you with insightful information to start a YouTube channel from scratch. Even if you have little to no experience, this book will assist you to master all the basic concepts.

We also highlight some challenges that new YouTubers face when they join the platform to equip you with the resilience that you need as you approach the competitive world on YouTube.

YouTube channels are more than information hubs; they are money-making opportunities! However, your ability to make more money through a YouTube channel depends on your consistency in implementing strategies that we will explore in this book. To be forewarned is to be forearmed. Brace yourself and build the confidence that you need to get your share of the money in the pool.

Chapter 1:

Finding a Niche for Your YouTube Channel

One of the first things that you will need to decide on before starting your YouTube channel is your niche. In general, the term "niche" describes the subject or topics that your channel will concentrate on, often referred to as genres or subgenres. You can also approach a niche by deciding on an "umbrella topic" and narrowing it down or choosing subtopics for your channel. For example, you could look at gardening as your umbrella topic. From there, you can break it down into subtopics like "building garden furniture" and "garden planning for beginners".

To be successful as a YouTuber, you will need to find a topic or subtopic that you will be known for. While this is a matter of passion and creativity, you will also need as many views as possible for you to make money from your channel. In this chapter, we will guide you through choosing the niche for your channel. We will also discuss various other factors that are associated with selecting the best niche for your channel.

Why Choosing a Niche Is Important

Before we start exploring how you can zero in on one niche for your YouTube channel, it is vital for us to discuss why taking this step is crucial. This will help you to attain a sense of purpose as you take on the procedure for selecting the best possible YouTube niche.

It's a Great Way to Get the YouTube Algorithm to Your Side

We will briefly explain how YouTube algorithms work so that you can take advantage of them in making your videos become popular.

Approximately 70% of the views that videos get on YouTube are aided by the platform's recommendation algorithm.

An algorithm is a loop for data collection, which uses the accumulated information to recommend videos to YouTube users. The data is collected from channels and viewers so that the algorithm can determine the audience who is more likely to be interested in certain types of videos. Therefore, if the algorithm does not pick your videos for recommendation to potential viewers, your progress might be compromised.

When you identify a niche for your content, you put your videos in a better position for being picked by the algorithm. You will also appear to be an expert in the subject area that you are dealing with. Once a first-time viewer who came across your video via algorithmic recommendations on YouTube enjoys your content, it is more likely that they may then search for your other content. The effect of this is that you will get more views and, of course, more money.

You Create Credibility That Enhances Engagement

In this era where everyone seems so busy, keep in mind that the majority of the people who are visiting YouTube might be looking for something specific. This could be games, cooking recipes, specific movies, comedies, you name it. So, imagine a scenario where someone is looking for the best way to make cakes on YouTube. They get to your channel because your first video is probably about a spongy cake. Let's suppose that they enjoy your content but the next time they look for your channel, they find that you are talking about pets. They may be put off and seek another channel that has consistent and relevant content.

Narrowing down to a certain niche displays a level of consistency that enhances better engagement with viewers. Your audience knows that the probability of finding what they are looking for is high on your channel. The more they find the answers that they are looking for on your channel, the more they are likely to stick around. The more time viewers spend on your channel, the higher the chances are that they will like or subscribe to your channel.

Simply put, the audience on YouTube is looking for channels that will give them what they are looking for with certainty, without having to jump from one channel to another. Attract them by focusing on a niche and then provide quality content that will keep them glued to your channel.

The Art of Finding Your Niche

The best niche is the one that you are passionate about and its ability to accumulate many views. The two factors tend to work together. If you are passionate about something that is unlikely to attract the attention of the targeted audience, then this might be a drawback, based on the business side. While there is a niche for everyone, it must be noted that some niches are either too controversial or outdated, or even ahead of the curve to have a decent enough following to be successful.

On the other hand, there are some subjects that you might not really be passionate about, but may be highly knowledgeable about. If that niche can yield many views, then it might be lucrative enough to consider. In this section, we will look at other factors that you may consider in picking the best niche for your channel.

Go for a Niche Within a Niche

Some niches are quite broad and may be difficult to establish a loyal audience in. While the general target audience might have a broad and common interest, there are some things that will separate them. If they find a more specific channel, then they will leave yours if it is too broad. For example, if your niche is comedy, you are probably trying to target everyone.

However, people don't find humor in the same things. Therefore, narrowing your niche a bit more and specifying the types of jokes that your channel will focus on is a great idea. For example, you could zero in on jokes on the experience of being a new employee or training a hyper dog to walk on a leash. This way, your audience knows the type of jokes that they should look forward to when they get to your channel.

Another popular "umbrella topic" is a "tech" channel. However, narrowing it down to a tech channel that focuses on personal audio equipment or reviewing fitness gadgets makes it the perfect destination for like-minded people to find your content.

Analyze the Viewer's Needs

Sometimes, taking some time to analyze and observe the viewing trends of the people that visit your channel gives you a better direction. For instance, you might see that there are some videos that attract more views than others. Consider concentrating more on the content that the audience loves more and give them better quality on that. Work on proving yourself to be an expert in the subject area and the likely rise in the number of views will amaze you.

Take Niche Competition Into Consideration

Imagine how fierce the competition will be when you create a YouTube channel in a niche that has channels with millions of subscribers and videos with millions of views. Some channel visitors check the previous views before they decide to watch the uploaded content. Based on this fact, such viewers are less likely to click the link to a channel that has just started streaming.

We recommend that you carefully do your research and look for niches that have relatively less competition. The chances that you will excel there are higher. Directly competing with a seasoned content creator who has been around for some time can make the initial phase of your channel more difficult.

There are some subjects that people are interested in, yet there are only a few videos that focus on them. In some cases, the few available videos do not present the quality that the audience is looking for. That's a gap that needs to be filled and you can be the one to get that done. In essence, choosing the right niche also requires some market research, just like any other business. Therefore, that idea that you think might not work simply because no one else is talking about it on YouTube could be your ticket to a successful YouTubing experience.

Go for a Sustainable Niche

You certainly don't want to get to a point where you run out of ideas on what to post just a few months down the line. This will disrupt the momentum at which you were growing your audience. To avoid such a situation, find a niche that will keep loads of work at your disposal. Dealing with seasonal subjects may see you facing sustainability issues. The gaps between the seasons will halt your YouTube channel for some time and by the time you come back, your audience might have been accommodated in another channel. You will keep starting over and over again, a scenario that is not healthy for your channel.

Never Underestimate the Power of Passion

Creating content on YouTube has its own ups and downs. One of the things that will carry you through the dips along the way is passion. To what extent are you passionate about the subject that you are screening? Without passion, your content creation tasks feel awful, so you won't look forward to the process. Another reason why passion is important in selecting a niche is that it shows clearly to your audience. They can see the excitement that you have as you talk about the topic, and this is enough to attract them and keep them glued to your channel.

Do Quality Research

Research is golden if you want to explore any new endeavor because it assists you to make informed decisions. With enough research, you can start on a high note within a niche that matches your interests, passion, and financial quest. Once you have an idea of your prospective niche, dig up information about the type of content that your fellow YouTubers are adding.

Find out why the audience is interested in such content. Moreover, find out how these YouTubers manage to keep the viewers engaged, in addition to making them regular visitors. If you go through the comments that the viewers add, you might find interesting pointers to areas of improvement. These will enlighten you on three major aspects, which are:

- the additions that you could possibly make to the subject at hand.

- insights on value addition.

- different perspectives for presenting the same thing.

Niche Options on YouTube

Another possible strategy that you can employ in identifying the best niche for your channel is learning about different niches that are trending on YouTube. Once you understand what happens in each niche, you can weigh the options and come up with the best possible option. To make things easier for you, we have compiled the various niches that currently get an excellent number of views:

- **Cooking:** Cooking is one of the most sustainable niches that YouTube will ever hold. This is because we all cannot do without food. Moreover, the abundance of food has increased the need to find out more recipes to make the eating experience more enjoyable. Cooking niches provide tips on how to come up with various food textures, appearances, flavors, and tastes.

- **How it is made:** Have you ever looked at a certain manufactured product and wondered how it was made? Many people have the curiosity to understand the manufacturing process of things. Their desire is quenched by the "how it is made" niche. Channels in this niche provide step-by-step processes of how things are made.

- **Beauty:** Many beauty videos focus on make-up and skincare, which involves showcasing products, techniques and trends.

With the consistent change in trends and products, and the techniques involved in applying them, the beauty niche is a sustainable one. *Shaaanxo* and *Jaclyn Hill* are some of the popular YouTube channels in the beauty niche; you could join them in this money-making venture!

- **Do it yourself (DIY):** There are so many things that we buy that we could, otherwise, make on our own. Making such things using your hands is much easier using guidance from videos that are found on YouTube. If you have some skills and tricks for making, say, bags, mats, toys, and other things, you can try the DIY niche.

- **How to:** The videos on this niche are meant to enlighten viewers on how to do certain things. Virtually anything that you can think of can be demonstrated through YouTube videos, from how to use certain equipment to simple tasks such as tricks for giving your hair a curled appearance. The "5-minute repair" is a good example of a DIY niche.

- **Gaming:** In this niche, instructions on how to properly play a trending new game are provided. You can also get insights on older games as well. The instructions on how to play the games range from beginner, through intermediate, to expert levels.

- **Life hacks:** This niche provides video tutorials that inform viewers about various alternatives to doing things. These alternatives are usually more efficient and quicker, and so they help the YouTube audience to save their time and money on certain tasks.

- **Comedy:** We all need just a laugh at one point or another. It takes a good and well-planned screening to lighten a bad mood and a stressful day. You could be one of such YouTube comedians if you have what it takes!

- **Fashion:** People cannot do away with fashion so channels that focus on this topic always have many viewers. Fashion is a broad niche that covers various clothing items, how to combine them, various color combinations, and so on. Getting down to a sub-niche could help you to create a more specific channel.

For example, you could choose to concentrate on bags or shoes.

- **Ask me anythings (AMAs):** In channels that fall under this niche, viewers can pose questions to celebrities. These questions are then answered via short videos, by the celebrities themselves. The whole purpose of doing this is to get information that is related to questions that only celebrities can answer. Considering there are limitations with regard to content, there are only a few channels in this niche.

- **Pranks:** Think of those things that make you exclaim and shout, "Oops!" or "That was close!" Like jokes, harmless pranks can enlighten our moments. If you can come up with such pranks, you can create a channel that is likely to get a lot of engagement, possibly from a younger audience.

- **Minecraft videos:** Minecraft is a video game where players are exposed to a world with building blocks, so they use cubes to create statues and castles. The building can be done in either a creative or survival mode. The majority of visitors to Minecraft videos are young people who enjoy playing the game, but it's important to note that there is a large audience of older viewers who may be interested in Minecraft videos as well.

- **Vlogs:** Vlogs is short for video logs. They describe personal diaries that are presented in the form of videos, highlighting aspects such as experiences, travels, or even daily activities. Through vlogs, one can learn how others run their lives or certain things. For instance, those who are interested in knowing and understanding Chinese lifestyles can search for vlogs by Chinese people.

- **Meal preparation day:** This niche serves people who are looking for healthy recipes that can keep extra calories away so that they become healthy and beautiful. Here, the channels expose the viewers to a variety of healthy ways of preparing their food. After trying the recipes, the viewers may also give feedback to help others.

- **Languages:** From the time when the COVID-19 pandemic was at its peak, connections between people of different languages and cultures relatively increased. This made the need to learn other languages more beneficial as it assists people to understand cultural diversity. However, learning a new language is not only difficult, but it is also a time-consuming effort. Channels in the language niche on YouTube make it easier for interested individuals to learn the basics of different languages. You can start your channel in this niche if you are good with languages.

Tips for Becoming Successful in Your Niche

Now that you have chosen the niche that is most appealing to you, the next important question is "How can I be successful?" Selecting the right niche is not enough. There are further steps that you should take to position your YouTube channel for better success. In this section, we will outline some tips that, if you consider and properly implement them, could see you getting more views and earnings.

Identify the Goal of the Channel

Just like any other business, your channel should have a mission. This is what we are referring to as a goal. Different channels in one niche may have varying goals. For example, in the cooking niche, some may focus on pastry only, while some are all about healthy foods. Some channels in the food niche may just talk about the food without practically showcasing how to prepare different dishes. All these variations are due to the goals that the channels have.

Focusing on one goal further helps to narrow down your niche so that you target a specific audience. It becomes easier for people to know what your channel is all about. Having a clear goal gives your videos a clear direction. Let's take the example of the 'unboxing' channel. On a channel like this, the presenter unboxes different products and analyzes them. The goal of this channel is to give the audience access to unbiased views that assist them to make informed decisions during purchases. When viewers go to a channel like this, they know what to expect.

To determine the goal for your channel, sincerely answer the question, "What do I intend to achieve by creating this channel?" Furthermore, ask yourself the following questions:

- Do you just want to provide information to the viewers?

- Do you want them to learn how to do things, step-by-step?

- What emotions are you targeting?

- Do you want the audience to be happy, empathetic, angry, or surprised?

Questions such as this help to give your goal some remarkable depth. Your content becomes less varied and that's a great strategy for attracting the right people, who are more likely to stick around for as long as the channel exists.

Create a Good Name for your Channel

This name should be easy to remember, and it is better when it relates to the type of content that you will stream on your channel. While there is no specific way of creating a name for your channel, there are some pointers that might be helpful. For instance, you can choose a name that:

- **Builds your personal brand:** This mainly applies if your videos revolve around your online persona. For example, you can use your first and last name for your channel if your videos are talk shows. Using your name for the name of your channel avoids limitations in terms of content. Think of Kelly Stamps. Her channel talks about many things, including making money, minimalism, and traveling.

- **Includes relevant keywords:** If your videos talk about topics that are searchable, using keywords increases the likelihood of being successful. For example, if you are streaming on topics like "How to make a shampoo from plants," you need to take note of the search words that viewers are more likely to use in looking for videos. Compile these words and weave them into a name for your channel.

- **Is original and unique:** Stealing other people's names is against YouTube regulations. Therefore, always create a name that doesn't impersonate other channels.

- **Adheres to YouTube's community guidelines:** YouTube stipulates words that are not allowed on their platform, so you should avoid them when you create the name of your channel.

Know Your Audience

Who are the people targeted by your content? You should define the characteristics that describe them. In other words, you should create an audience persona. The imagined character with the attributes that describe your ideal viewer is what we are calling the audience persona. Having your audience persona will assist you to create content that matches the needs and availability of your target audience. Here are some questions that may come in handy in creating that ideal audience that you wish to serve through your content:

- Who is more likely to watch your videos?

- Why should they be interested in your videos?

- How old is the targeted audience?

- Are they employed or not? If yes, what are their job descriptions?

- What does their daily schedule look like?

- Around what time will they watch your videos?

Plan on Providing Content Consistently

YouTubers who are successful upload content consistently. Your audience should know when to expect your new video. Inconsistency kills the viewers' interest in your channel.

You can ensure that you regularly add videos to your channel by creating a content schedule. This way, you can also plan your work in a more organized manner, so it is easier to stay on track. It would be awesome if you could upload content on a daily basis but it's also crucial to consider the sustainability of your content schedule.

For instance, adding content to your channel every day can be overwhelming in the long run, especially if you are currently working alone on your projects. A weekly schedule where you create one video every week is a good start. As you get more accustomed to the process, you can start adding content, say, two times a week.

For example, a good recipe is to upload content every Saturday at a time that your viewers will be online to see it. To keep the audience in the loop, you have to make sure the schedule is clearly mentioned on your banners. Consistency is a magnet for more views.

Acquire Quality Equipment

You certainly want to make sure that the content that you upload on your channel is of excellent quality. The best way to ensure this is by using quality equipment. Please note that we are not insinuating that you should purchase expensive equipment right from the beginning. However, you need equipment that will give your channel a good starting point, in terms of quality.

There are just a few basics that you will require, and these are:

- **Computer:** The speed should be decent enough not to slow you down.

- **Video editing software:** iMovie, Movie Maker, Corel VideoStudio, and Filmora are some of the inexpensive options that you can consider. Depending on the capital that is available to you, there are even more options.

- **Screen recorder:** You won't go wrong with the Debut Screen Recorder. It is inexpensive and it also allows you to add captions to the videos that you make.

- **Camera:** If you intend to create your videos beyond screen recording, then you will need a camera. If you have a high-end camera phone, there is no harm in starting with your smartphone camera.

- **Microphone:** Do your videos require you to speak? If yes, then you need a good microphone. The videos that you make will be judged partly on the sound.

Don't Forget Channel Optimization

Remember, there are millions of channels that are available on YouTube. Therefore, you need to employ strategies that make yours appear at the top when people search for things that are related to your content. This is where optimization comes in. You can make use of the "About" section on your channel to enlighten your readers about the type of content that you focus on. Please note that readability is very important when you do this. Avoid long sentences and fluff that do not add value to your explanation. Remember, some of the people who will read that information are quite busy so go straight to the point to keep them engaged.

To further optimize your channel, be sure to use certain keywords when you write the description for your "About" section. Make sure that these words fit in the flow of the sentences and paragraphs so that they don't sound awkward. Are you wondering what we are referring to by the term "keywords"? When you go on YouTube in search of certain information, there are certain words that you type in the search box.

YouTube then gives you the best possible channels based on the words that you would have typed. Similarly, keywords are those words or phrases that your target audience is more likely to use when they search for your content. To identify such words, ask yourself, "Which words would I possibly use if I wanted to search for...?"

Here are more ideas for optimizing your channel:

- Be sure to use the keywords about four times in your description in the "About" section.

- Go through discussions on platforms like Quora so that you get to know the hot topics and the vocabulary used.

- Use the Google Keyword planner or Ahrefs, both of which are keyword research tools that help you to identify common queries that you can use for creating videos that attract news.

Learn From Your First Video Upload

From the list of content ideas that you have, pick one of the best ones to entice viewers. If done well, this video will earn you your first set of loyal viewers. As the number of views builds up, this will attract even more people to watch your videos. However, remember it's your first try and so perfection won't be impossible. Don't hit yourself for things that do not go well because they present an opportunity to learn and get better.

According to the quote by Alvin Toffler, "The illiterate of the 21st century will not be those who cannot read and write, but those who cannot learn, unlearn, and relearn". This quote also applies to being a successful YouTuber. You should be willing to *learn* completely new things, *unlearn* things that don't seem to work and *relearn* even the things that you think you already know.

Check the comments and see what people are happy about and take note of their complaints. Do not turn off comments just because you don't like the negative ones. Once potential viewers get to a channel that has comments that are turned off, they might lose their trust. YouTube Analytics is an important tool for assessing the extent to which your video was able to retain viewers. You can use it and apply the results in improving your videos.

Keep Up With the Changes in Your Niche

Considering the possible competition that might be in your niche, you should strive to be seen as the most knowledgeable. This is why you should remain up-to-date with the latest developments in your niche. Listen to news, talk to relevant people, and make observations, just to get hold of something new. Searching for what's new in your niche is a viable strategy for feeding your audience with fresh content regularly.

Implement Proper Community Engagement

The moment we talk about engaging your channel's community, the first thing that probably comes into your mind is liking and responding to the audience's comments. You can go a step further by hosting a live stream on YouTube. This gives you an opportunity to directly engage and converse with your audience. You can also use live streaming when you take on question-and-answer sessions.

This is another awesome way to keep your audience involved in growing your channel. The viewers can ask you questions while you answer them in real time. You can also ask them to write down their questions in the comments section so that you can address them in subsequent videos. Mind you, their questions may give insights for content ideas because then you know what people are looking for.

You can also engage with your audience beyond the YouTube platform. Doing this shows the commitment that you have toward the community that is served by your videos. Moreover, this strategy also allows you to entice new audiences. Some of the platforms that you can consider are Facebook, LinkedIn, and X.

More practices for growing your community are outlined below:

- Always make an announcement on all your other platforms when you are about to release a new video on YouTube.

- When you upload a new video, be sure to add a link that directs the audience to the previous one.

- Create an online forum where conversations about your content and other related aspects can continue.

- Start a blog for your content.

- You could consider a podcast where you present your ideas differently.

To ensure that you have taken the right steps in ensuring that you have oriented yourself for success on YouTube, we created checklists that you can tick as you go. This will assist in making sure that you are on the right track. The first table assesses how you have chosen the niche for your channel. The second one evaluates the extent to which you have implemented the strategies for making your channel successful. In both tables, place a tick under the column that best describes the prompts.

Please note that in each niche on YouTube, you will find stellar content creators who consistently produce content that is well-received by their audience. People connect with who they are and the authenticity of their content. Strive to learn from such YouTubers and be geared for success. In this chapter, we focused on how to choose a niche for your channel. We also guided you on how you can be successful after selecting your niche. Assuming that you now have a niche in mind, the next chapter will take you through the "how part" of setting up and managing your YouTube channel.

Checklist

	Conduct research about niches you are interested in.
	Ensure that the content in your mind matches the viewers' needs.
	Determine whether the niche(s) is/are sustainable.
	Identify and evaluate the competition.
	Ensure the niche is driven by passion and creativity.

Identify the goal for the channel.
Create a good name.
Identify an audience persona.
Devise a rough content schedule and determine if you can provide consistent content.
Ensure you have good quality equipment.
Identify gaps and areas of improvement.
Engage your community.

Chapter 2:

Setting Up and Managing Your YouTube Channel

In this chapter, we will delve into the technical aspects of creating your YouTube channel. We will also discuss how to manage your channel like a pro. Setting up and managing your channel the proper way contributes much to your success as a content creator on YouTube. The tips that we will provide in this chapter will see you approach the beginnings and progress of your business with enhanced ease and confidence.

Step-By-Step Guide for Creating a YouTube Channel

As you go through some of the videos on YouTube, you might wonder how the people in charge of the channels get started. While it appears so complicated from a distance, once you have all the information, you will see that it is something that you can do. Interestingly, this section was put together to give you that "I can do it" kind of perception. We will outline the steps that you should take to create your YouTube channel so that you can start putting your content out there.

Step 1: Create a Google Account

YouTube is owned by Google, which is why you need a Google account for you to create a channel on YouTube. If you have already been using Google Maps, Gmail, or Google Play, then you already have a Google account. However, we do not recommend that you use your personal Google account for creating your YouTube channel. Rather create another Google account that is solely for your business. The advantage of taking this move is that a business Google account makes it possible for other people to manage your YouTube account without peeping into your personal emails.

That brings us to another question, "Is it not possible to use your personal Google account and still protect your emails?" It is quite possible, just that there are extra steps that you should take that you could avoid by just creating a separate business Google account. You can make sure that other people who you work with do not have access to your personal emails by using the permission settings functionality.

To create a Google account that is dedicated to your business, go to Google and search for "create a Google account." The link from the search results will take you to a page where you should fill in details and follow the prompts. Basically, you will need to enter your first and last names and email address, then create your password. Please note that this step is only necessary if you don't already have a business account. Also, the names and email addresses that you enter will not be publicly linked to your business brand.

Step 2: Create the Channel

The moment you create a Google account, a personal YouTube account is assigned to you. Now, go to your YouTube account or simply search for YouTube.com in your browser. On the far right, you will see an icon for your profile, click it. At the top of the drop-down menu, click "**My Channel**." This action will then take you to a page where you are given the option to choose the name that you will use for the channel.

Click "**Use a business or other name**" and this will take you to a page where you can fill in your business name, against the prompt that says, "Brand Account name." It is possible to change the business name later on if need be. Select "**Create**." The moment you do this, you will be taken to a page that allows you to customize your channel if you want to. Choose "**Customize channel**" on the available options.

Step 3: It's Time to Customize

There are three aspects of your channel that you can customize, and these are the "About section," the channel icon, and art. These steps give your channel a unique touch and brand that sets it apart from other channels in the same niche.

Channel Icon

This is what you would call the profile image, especially if it was a personal account. You can put your logo as the icon for your channel. There is no harm in placing your image there, as long as that's how you want to present your channel to the YouTube world. Please note that you should use the 800 x 800 px dimensions for the image of your choice.

To add the icon for your channel, hover your mouse on the channel placeholder that is brown in color. A pencil icon will appear and when you click on it, you will get options for uploading the image of your choice. Follow the prompts and add the image that will represent your brand.

When you add your icon, here are some of the nuggets that you should keep in mind:

- Make sure the icon remains clear when it's zoomed in or out.

- YouTube does circle cropping on your image, so the corners are cut off. Therefore, be sure to position the icon in such a way that even after the cropping procedure, it remains clear.

Channel Art

You can think of this as the cover photo on platforms such as Facebook that spans a larger area than the channel icon. You are not obliged to add the channel art but adding it adds some vibe to the page. The default image is dull and can be boring to your audience.

Be careful of your choice of the image that you add to the channel art. It is preferable for you to use an image that relates well with your brand. This way, your audience will know that they are not lost just by seeing the channel art on your page. Ideally, the channel art image should be 2,560 x 1,440 px. You can add your channel art by simply clicking "Add channel art," prior to following the prompts. If you desire channel art with enhanced quality, you can use tools like Canva.

Please note that you can still come back and add the channel art at a later stage. At this stage, your aim is to make sure that the channel is set and ready for business. Therefore, to avoid wasting much time, you can just add a solid color as a placeholder for your channel art. Make sure the color that you add matches those that represent your brand.

The "About" Section

This section is a brief description of what your channel is all about. Format it into paragraphs that are shorthand and straightforward. As we mentioned in the previous chapter, remember to add some keywords to your description. These keywords could be the topics that you will include in your channel or any other search words that your audience might use in looking for content. Also, be sure to list the email address and website for your company so that the audience can connect and get in touch with you.

Step 4: Add Channel Managers

If there are other people who are working with you and you want them to be involved in managing the channel, you can add them as managers. To add managers, click on the channel profile, and then select "Settings" from the drop-down menu. This will take you to a page where you can choose "Add or remove managers."

You will then be taken to another page where you can click on the blue button that says, "Manage Permissions." A pop box will appear and at the top right corner, you will see an icon, click on it. Your name will already be there. You can then add the email addresses of every individual who will manage the YouTube channel with you. An invitation will be sent to the email addresses that you would have added.

Step 5: Add Your First Video

Once you have the first video that you want to share with the world, make sure you save it in a folder that is easily accessible. You could consider saving your video in "Downloads," "Documents," or on "Desktop." Now, go to your YouTube account. At the top right corner, click on "Create." Follow the prompts. At some point, you will be asked to upload your files. Access your saved video and continue following the instructions.

Step 6: Make the Channel Easier to Find

With the billions of channels that are available on YouTube, you will need to ensure that your own stands out. This is why you should do everything possible to enhance the ease at which it can be found by interested individuals. This is done by optimizing the video.

The first step in optimizing your video is filling in responses to the prompts that are on the "Details" screen. On this screen, you will be required to enter the title of your video, as well as its description and a thumbnail. A picture that acts as a preview of what is in your video is what we are referring to as the thumbnail. It has to be captivating enough to lure potential viewers into clicking on your video. There are also functionalities that allow you to add other video elements like an end screen and subtitles.

Another important strategy for optimizing your videos is by using keywords. To find out the best keywords for your content, tools such as TubeBuddy and VidIQ will certainly come in handy.

Step 7: Customize the Layout and Bring Out the Vibe

Once you have one, two, or more videos uploaded on your channel, get ready to customize its appearance so that it exudes the feel that you desire. A good layout helps you to capture viewers so that they stick around for longer on your channel. If you want to make changes to the layout of your channel, go to the "Customize Channel" page.

On the top navigation bar on that page, select the menu and then click "Layout." Doing this will expose you to two options, which are "Featured sections" and "Video spotlight." Click on these options and follow the prompts to make the changes that you want.

It is possible to adjust your channel's settings so that the content that the viewers see depends on their subscribing status. For instance, you could add featured videos for loyal subscribers. For those who are yet to subscribe, you can show a channel trailer. Ideally, potential viewers could be more interested in knowing what your channel is all about, which is why a video that provides a comprehensive overview is a great idea. A returning viewer who is already a subscriber wouldn't necessarily need such information. Therefore, a featured video might be a better idea.

Step 8: Develop an Organized Playlist

Through a playlist, you can compile videos that are similar and allow them to play in a continuous manner and with coherence. For instance, you can identify videos that have similar topics and group them into a playlist. One of the advantages of a playlist is that it keeps your channel's audience engaged so they are more likely to spend more time watching your content.

The more the viewers spend quality time on your channel, the higher the chances that they become more connected to your brand. They even get to understand it better. Besides, playlists save your viewers' time because they can find your videos without having to search for them separately.

You can create a playlist in a few simple steps. Begin by clicking the menu on the left-hand side of the screen. After that, click "Playlist" on the menu, and select "New Playlist," which is positioned at the far top of the right part of the screen. You can then name the playlist that you are about to create. You also retain the leverage to determine the visibility level of your playlist.

Now that you have set up the playlist, it's time to add the videos. Check the left-hand side of the screen and select "Content." You can then click the new playlist and start adding videos to it. There you go; your playlist is ready!

Hardware and Software Needed

The steps that we described in the previous section can only be completed if you have the right equipment and software at your disposal. This might not necessarily mean that you need sophisticated equipment that is possibly very expensive. You can start where you are and rise as you go. Find out what equipment and software you require for you to get started on your journey to becoming a successful YouTuber.

Camera

While you might be tempted to use an old camera or something similar, a smartphone might give you better results than you might have imagined. This could be your Android or Apple device, as long as the quality of the videos that it produces is not less than 1,080 pixels. It's a great way to get started while you build up your audience base.

As you begin to grow your business, you will notice the need to upgrade the type of camera that you use, in a bid to produce content of better quality. When that time comes, you may need to get a camera. Please note that the type of camera that you need is highly dependent on the nature of the content that you intend to deliver on YouTube. Let's look at some types that you may choose from:

- **The camcorder:** Camcorders are designed for resting videos, so they are a great option for creating your content. Other advantages that come with this type of camera are that they are relatively lighter, more affordable, compact, and flexible enough to create videos, despite the situation. Whether you are home or traveling, a camcorder is applicable. If you need a camcorder and you are working on a limited budget, you can go for the Sony HDR-CX405 camcorder, whose price is approximately

$250. Another good option is the Panasonic HC-V180K, which goes for about $180.

- **The webcam:** This camera is better applicable for plug-and-play case scenarios. In other words, if you prefer a camera that you can plug into your computer and start recording, the webcam is probably what you need. This partly explains why the webcam camera works well for gaming YouTubers. This camera also comes in handy if you need to engage in live streaming because you can simply connect your camera to the computer. One of the good webcam options that you may want to consider is the Logitech C922 Pro Stream. This camera has a resolution of 1080p, and it is supportive of 760 px and 60 fps streaming. You can get the Logitech C922 Pro Stream at around $74. The Razer Kiyo also works well and has the same resolution as the Logitech C922 Pro Stream. However, you can buy the former at a lower price of approximately $60.

- **The action camera:** Are you looking for a camera that displays remarkable versatility, especially when you are capturing some action? The action might be what you are looking for. Action cameras come in small sizes so they can be easily carried around. Besides that, these cameras are currently the best when it comes to quality. A good example of an action camera is the GoPro HERO10 Black, which you can get for around $350.

- **Mirrorless cameras:** If you are looking for a camera that is as close to a DSLR as possible, you might need to have a look at mirrorless cameras. These cameras are also relatively smaller and lighter, compared to the DSLR. With mirrorless cameras, you can capture your videos in the comfort of your home or office, or while you are on the move. The Panasonic Lumix GH6 Mirrorless Camera Body is a mirrorless camera whose costs are around $1,700.

- **DSLR:** The high-quality videos that are produced by DSLR certainly give your YouTube business the boost to take off. This type of camera also adapts well to conditions of low light without compromising quality. This gadget is quite pricey but purchasing it is an investment that you will not regret, especially if you are a YouTube content creator. One of the good DSLR cameras that is worth mentioning is the Canon EOS Rebel SL3. You can get this camera at a cost of $749.

The External Microphone

If you are one of the people who read comments by other viewers before watching a video, you might have come across statements like, "The sound is terrible" or "Some parts of the video are barely audible." Such comments are a reflection of poor sound, and you wouldn't want to fall into the same trap when creating your videos. No matter how awesome the picture quality of your video is, it can be nullified by bad sound.

This causes viewers to lose interest in your channel. To avoid this, you should invest in an external microphone. Just like the cameras, you should know the external microphone that meets your needs. Let's explore some of the available options below:

- **USB microphones:** Some of the good characteristics of USB microphones are good sound quality, versatility, ease of use, and affordability. Many YouTubers find these microphones quite useful in their line of business. The Logitech Clearchat Headset is a beginner-friendly USB microphone that you can get for around $30.

- **Condenser microphone:** When you are using a condenser microphone, you won't require a pre-amp. The microphone has a built-in headphone jack, alongside the volume control. It also has the functionality for mixing pre-recorded audio with your microphone audio. If you want a condenser microphone, the Audio-Technica AT2020USB Plus is an option that you could consider.

- **Shotgun microphone:** Shotgun microphones are laced with portability and the ability to produce high-quality videos. This microphone also has shock mounts that assist with reducing the noise from the vibrations that take place around it. Another unique attribute of the shotgun microphone is its ability to focus on capturing the voice that is right in front of it while avoiding any ambient noise around the gadget. You can buy the Rode Microphones VideoMic Pro R, as it works very well with a mirrorless camera, DSLR, or camcorder.

- **Lapel microphone:** The lapel microphone is also referred to as the lavalier mic. It is wireless so you can simply clip it on your clothes or accessories such as belts. The receiver of this type of microphone can be very effective in picking up sounds, even from a distance. If you are in love with the lapel microphone, you can purchase the Rode Wireless GO II Compact Microphone System.

Gimbal Stabilizer or Tripod

You certainly don't want to have videos that are wavy and unstable, especially if you want to appear professional. This is why you need a tool that can stabilize your videos and photos. Gimbal stabilizers or tripods have this functionality.

- **Tripod:** Tripods are three-legged stands for your camera. You can get these affordable stands at less than $100. When you choose a tripod, be sure to get one that is durable and strong enough to keep your equipment secure from falling. You can try the iKan E-Image EG01A2 whose quality and costs are quite commendable.

- **Gimbal stabilizer:** Gimbals have some weights that are meant to give them some balance. When you then mount your camera, this tool remains stable even when you make huge movements. This is especially necessary if you are using a lightweight camera. If you intend to use lightweight mirrorless cameras, the DJI Ronin-SC is a commendable choice.

Lighting Equipment

If you are going to record your videos indoors, where the environment is relatively dim, you will need additional lighting to brighten the spaces. Even in spaces that seem to have adequate light, professional lighting tools can help to even out the lighting, making it more appropriate. Therefore, managing your lighting significantly contributes to the quality of your YouTube videos. In this section, we will explore some of the lighting equipment that is worth noting.

- **Softbox:** If your videos require light that is not accompanied by harsh shadows, then you need a softbox among your tools. This equipment can diffuse direct and harsh light, thereby reducing its intensity. This way, the softbox can imitate the natural form of lighting that comes through a window. This tool is a great way of controlling the lighting around your videos. For a start, consider buying the CLAR SoftBox because it works well for indoor video shootings.

- **Ring light:** Vloggers tend to prefer this lighting equipment. The ring emits some light around the focus area. The positive effect of this is the elimination of shadows that may affect the quality of the video. With ring lights, your videos will appear attractive and professional. Blemishes are hidden. One of the best options for ring lights is the Flashpoint 19-inch ring light. This ring light's heat emission is low and reasonable so there is no harm in placing it closer to the focal point, where the subject is.

- **On-camera lighting:** When on-camera lights are mounted on a camera, they provide continuous light that is necessary when you are filming events such as weddings. This type of lighting also comes in handy when you make videos in dim spaces. If your channel focuses on documentaries, on-camera lighting is a great option. One such lighting tool is the iKan iLED-MA Micro Flood Light.

Software for Editing Your Videos

Using your best picks for hardware, you can produce good videos on the go. However, you will still need to edit your video until you get the finished product that you desire. You will need some video editing software to get this done. YouTube does have its own video editing software but getting yours is a very good idea. This way, you can have greater leverage to make as many modifications to your video as you would like.

If you are wondering where to start, you could consider Adobe Premiere Elements 2022. This video editor has gained much preference among many photographers. It comes with many editing options, such as freeze frames, animations, trimming, and bounce-back effects. Other good options for video editing software include Shortcut, Apple iMovie, Final Cut Pro X, Filmora 9, and HitFilm Express.

Misconceptions About Starting Your YouTube Channel

When you scroll through some YouTube channels and see some channels with millions of views, what comes to your mind? You probably think that you can also easily do it right? However, from what you have learned from this book so far, you can attest that it's not really that easy. You have to put in some quality effort. Thinking that you can just wake up and make it in the YouTube business is one of the biggest misconceptions that many people have.

There are strategies and tricks that you need to master and that is why you have this book in your possession. In this section, we will look at even more misconceptions that are associated with starting a YouTube channel. Learning about these untrue notions will put you in a better position to separate between false ideas and noteworthy ones. Let's get the ball rolling!

You Will Make a Lot of Money in Little Time

It is true that you will make money with YouTube but probably not as fast as you might be thinking. For you to start making money from YouTube, you are expected to build a certain number of subscribers. It even looks like the standard number of subscribers that you are required to have is becoming higher with time. Now, it takes a lot of time for you to build a good number of loyal viewers. It takes effort, time, connections, and many other things. Therefore, as a beginner YouTuber, your main focus should be on connecting with viewers and creating a loyal subscriber base. Money will come along the way and when it does, you will enjoy the process even more.

Starting a YouTube Channel Is Expensive

Just a quick thought about starting a YouTube channel will make you think that the whole process is way too expensive. You might be weighing expenses in terms of money and time, but either way, being a YouTuber is not necessarily that demanding. From the description and explanations that we gave in the previous section, you can tell that starting a YouTube channel can be as cheap as possible.

In terms of time, creating videos does not require much of your time as it probably seems. You could set aside an average of three hours every week for creating your content. This isn't much, or is it? As you gain more experience in content creation, you might even set aside less time for creating your videos.

Your First Video Will Go Viral

Having your video go viral is a good thing, but the likelihood that this would happen on your first video is quite low. Please note that we are not saying that there is no way your first video can get viral—it could, but the chances are very low. When you start your channel, avoid raising your hopes too high when it comes to creating viral videos. Again, focus on making your channel better and more goal oriented.

Mind you, it might even take time for your videos to start appearing in YouTube searches. That shouldn't dishearten you. As long as you have clear and good ideas for your channel, keep posting more videos.

Companies Will Be Competing to Have You Review Their Products

If your channel focuses on reviewing products, don't entertain the daydream that companies will always send you things to review, for free. The reality might disappoint you. As you start out, you will need to buy things and then review them. Forget about receiving products for free, especially as you start out. The companies that offer goods to YouTube reviewers only do so to seasoned ones, because of the greater possibility of getting more clients.

So, to companies, having their products reviewed on YouTube is a marketing strategy. Therefore, for this to work, they have to give their products to YouTubers who already have many followers and are established enough to be heard by their audience.

Being a YouTuber Is for Extroverts

Both introverts and extroverts have equal chances of making it on YouTube. Remember, creating YouTube videos is not all about talking. You still radiate the energy that captures your viewers without having to say a single word. Of course, this would depend on the type of content that you produce on your channel. Just be creative, confident, and focused; your personality traits might not matter that much.

Your Videos Will Be More or Less the Same as Those of Your Model YouTuber

Interestingly, when you look at your favorite YouTubers' current videos, you forget that they also started from somewhere. It is even more likely that their first video was far from being good. So, when your first video doesn't look that great, don't feel discouraged. Remain focused and you will get to where your model YouTuber is someday. They will probably be on another stage by then but keep going.

YouTube Is Already Oversaturated

We cannot deny the fact that there are so many videos that are already available on YouTube right now. However, we do not agree that the platform is oversaturated. There is a lot that you do differently to make your videos stand out, even if you are talking about a subject that has been explored a thousand times. If you incorporate your personality, background, and creativity, your videos will be different from those of your competitors.

Do your research and look for possible gas in the niche. You will be surprised to see that there are thousands of alternatives for putting across the same message. Once you can grab just one of them, you will have your space on YouTube.

Technical Skills for Managing Your Channel

Being a YouTuber is more than just creating and uploading videos. There are a lot more things involved. The whole process becomes a success when you are able to put certain skills into play. Which skills are relevant for managing your YouTube channel? Let's find out in this section.

Research Skills

If you want to create excellent videos that are sought after by your target audience, it all starts with extensive research. The same applies if you want to find out the presentation strategy that appeals more to the people you are targeting. Without good research, it is difficult to create videos that can survive the massive competition that currently exists on the YouTube platform.

Good research skills help you to do a SWOT (**s**trengths, **w**eaknesses, **o**pportunities, and **t**hreats) analysis for evaluating the possible opportunities available. With the SWOT analysis, you can identify the strengths and weaknesses of your competitors. This helps you to maximize their weaknesses so that you get better at what they are not doing so well. If they are posing a possible threat to your upcoming business, find out how best you can nullify or manage the situation. All this is possible through extensive research.

Video Editing Skills

If we were to give identical complete videos to two different people and ask them to make edits as they deem fit, the results would bring an important point home. The editing results will obviously be different and sadly, one of the video products will be better than the other. The differences between the two edited videos will determine their acceptability to the target audience. Simply put, you should work on polishing your video editing skills. If you can't do it well on your own, it's important that you find someone who can assist you.

Social Media Skills

As a YouTuber, you should do everything possible to ensure that you feature on as many social media platforms as you can. Most of the people who you are more likely to find on YouTube are also affiliated with many other social media platforms. They can detect your seriousness when they see your brand more often, on various social media platforms. You even get more content ideas by just scrolling through social media. Social media platforms such as Facebook and X can help you make meaningful connections that may come in handy in growing your YouTube audience.

Graphic Designing Skills

Just imagine how you decide on the video to click on, after entering your search words on YouTube. You are more likely to check the thumbnails and then click on the ones that are more appealing to you. That is what your audience will also do, which is why graphic designing skills are relevant for you as a content creator. Please note that you don't necessarily need to be an expert graphic designer for you to create captivating thumbnails. You will be good enough with basic graphic designing abilities.

Marketing Skills

Good marketing skills are very important, considering that there might be millions of other YouTubers fighting for the same eyeballs as you. This type of skill makes it easier for viewers to come across your videos. Great marketing skills include the ability to write straightforward descriptions that contain appropriate keywords.

You should know how to manipulate tags in your title, to make the channel and the videos more searchable. Collaborating with other YouTubers can also be an effective way for marketing your content. This strategy helps to increase the size of the audience that can view your videos, thereby increasing your chances of success.

Video Production Skills

As you might have seen by now, the process of producing a video is, in itself, highly technical. You will need to understand more about aspects such as sound and set design, as these matter when it comes to the quality of your videos. You should also know how to manipulate the light around the spaces where you are taking your videos from. It is vital for you to know the type of equipment that works best for the type of content that you produce. It doesn't necessarily have to be expensive, but appropriate.

Channel Analytics Skills

This type of skill assists you to evaluate the progress of your channel. With channel analytics, you can determine what is working well and what isn't. One of the useful tools that you can use for such analyses is YouTube Studio. There are a lot of parameters that you can assess using this tool, which include:

- **Click-through rate (CTR):** This is presented as a percentage, and it represents the number of people who clicked on your video.

- **Audience retention:** This parameter assesses the extent to which the viewers watched your video. How many watched the complete video?

- **Subscribers gained:** How many people subscribed to your video?

- **Engagement levels:** This parameter evaluates the likes, comments, or shares for your videos.

- **Viewer statuses:** This assesses how many of the viewers are new against the returning ones.

Here is the chapter checklist that will help you keep in touch with what you learned. The first checklist is for the steps for creating your YouTube channel. The second one assesses your readiness by evaluating the equipment and technical skills that you already have. Present your responses by ticking the appropriate answer.

This chapter was meant to equip you with all the basics that you need to get started with your YouTube channel. Now that you generally have an idea of what is expected of you as a content creator on YouTube, the next chapter will guide you on how to create high-quality videos.

Checklist

	Invest in the right equipment: camera, microphone, lighting, stabilizer, editing software.
	Brush up on skills: research skills, marketing, social media, video production, graphic design, analytics, video editing.
	Film your first video and edit it.
	Create a Google account.
	Create a YouTube account and channel.
	Customize your channel.
	Add managers to your channel if relevant.
	Upload your first video as soon as you've created your channel.

	Customize the layout of your channel.
	Optimize your channel by using keywords so that viewers can find your channel easily.
	Create a playlist that your viewers will be interested in following.

Chapter 3:

Creating High-Quality Video Content

As you continue to add more videos to your channel, it's important that you focus on improving the quality of your content. At times, the quality of your videos may turn potential viewers away, even if you have interesting content. Another reason why you should strive to better your content is because of the fierce competition that you are more likely to face on YouTube.

When the quality of your videos is good, your chances of attracting loyal viewers and subscribers are relatively high. Some viewers may recommend your channel to others, thereby increasing your coverage. You also stand better chances of collaborating with other YouTubers when your videos are of good quality. No one wants to collaborate with someone whose quantity is not remarkable when it comes to content.

Steps for Creating Content on YouTube

Creating content on YouTube can be accompanied by a range of emotions—from excitement to confusion, especially if you are a beginner. However, you can be more confident with your work if you follow defined steps that show that you know what you are doing. This section will take you through four main steps for publishing your content on YouTube.

Step 1: Titles and Video Thumbnails

Viewers fall in love with thumbnails and titles before they get to the actual content. This means that these two can either attract or repel clicks for their YouTube audience. Therefore, once you are clear on the type of content that you want to create for your channel, be sure to create catchy titles and thumbnails.

Interestingly, you are allowed to change the thumbnails for your videos as you go. This means that if you see that one thumbnail is not working well, you can remove it and add another one. We, therefore, recommend that you create more than one thumbnail for each video that you create. Changing thumbnails can also help you to assess what the audience seems to like most. You can even replace thumbnails to match changing trends on YouTube as time progresses.

Characteristics of Good Thumbnails

Ideally, thumbnails should have the following properties:

- **Vivid and relevant images:** The pictures on your thumbnail should be visually clear and reflect the content in your video. For instance, it would be a good idea to use a thumbnail of flowers or a garden bed if your video is about flower gardening.

- **Basic and concise text:** Be straightforward and concise when you use text on your thumbnails. Remember to include your video's keywords so that your content is further optimized for YouTube's search engine.

- **Emotional captivation:** Humans are social beings and are empathetic. If you can reflect some emotions on your thumbnails, viewers may be more likely to click on your video. Faces that show emotions that reflect your video, like joy or surprise could be the way to go!

- **Attractive and appropriate colors:** The colors on your thumbnails should be vibrant compared to YouTube's backdrop. This will make it stand out but ensure that you are consistent with your brand color.

- **Instill curiosity:** Make sure your thumbnail plants curiosity in potential viewers, but be careful not to give out too much information. You want people to watch the video and not simply scroll past because they know what to expect from your video.

Titles are among the first points of contact between your videos and the audience. Make sure the titles have the following characteristics:

- They should be short, precise, informative, and visible.

- They should be an authentic reflection of the video content.

- They should include keywords that help your videos to be picked through search engine optimization (SEO).

Creating great titles for your videos is easier when you understand the problem that the video intends to solve for your viewers. People want to know why they should click your video so this strategy can be great bait. Going through the titles of other content creators in the same niche could also furnish you with better ideas.

Step 2: Create a Video Outline and Script

Creating an outline for your video is a great way of planning and organizing the content. An outline is simply a clear projection of the frame and flow of your video. We recommend that you write this down on your computer or on paper. A good outline helps you to reduce the chances of making avoidable mistakes in your video by adopting this strategy. With a well-made outline, you can easily determine what you need before you start making your video. This also means that you are less likely to waste time with too much trial and error.

Once you have your outline in place, go on and write down the actual script. Make it as informative as possible. Of course, your script is subject to modification where necessary so it's okay to allow it to be flexible. Please note that there are some types of videos that even work better without written scripts. Think of reaction videos—they can't really be planned, otherwise, they lose their vibe and goal.

Step 3: Filming, Editing, and Reviewing

You can regard steps 1 and 2 as pre-production stages. However, it is possible that you might, at this stage, discover that there is something that you missed out on during the first two preparation stages. That shouldn't discourage you. After all, you haven't put too many resources into your video yet. Simply restructure and strategize accordingly.

At times, you can see mistakes after shooting your video—that is fine, too. Reshoots are part of the process of content creation. Would you rather settle for a poor-quality video that doesn't represent your brand well than go for a reshoot and make things better? The latter is certainly the way to go.

After filming a video that you are happy with, the next step would be editing. If you are wondering what video editing entails, here are some ideas to keep in mind:

- Make sure your video clips are arranged in a correct order that flows well.

- If you need to add a voice-over, do so and make sure it synchronizes with the video.

- Are you happy with the colors on your footage? If not, there is an option to make adjustments using color grading.

- Adding intros and outros can be a great idea if you do it strategically. Otherwise, you might risk reducing viewer retention as some members of your audience might prefer going straight to the point.

- Add some screen text to aid information retention by your viewers.

- Cut off weird pauses and unnecessary pieces of footage.

- Incorporate transitions and cuts that add value to your video. Good examples include audio snippets, graphics, GIFs, and screenshots.

When you are done with your edits, you can find someone to review. A different pair of eyes can bring in new editing ideas and identify possible mistakes. Reviewing the edited version of your video can be done as many times as possible until you are happy with the result.

Step 4: Publish the Video on YouTube

It's time to publish your video on YouTube! As you add your video, remember to turn on closed captions. Doing this increases the accessibility of your video. Immediately follow up on the progress of your video for at least 24 hours. Based on its performance, you might need to switch thumbnails so that you give it a boost.

Creating Good Content on YouTube: The "Must-Know" Tips

Coming up with engaging content on YouTube is an art that requires creativity. You also need to plan your things well and be organized. In this section, we will explore some of the strategies that you can employ for you to create quality content for your channel.

Come Up With Goals for Your Channel

Once you have a channel and it's time to add content, you should be clear on your goals. You should know what your channel intends to achieve. Do you want to give your audience information? Do you want them to engage and buy the products or services that you are talking about on your channel? Are you introducing a certain product? What do you want your viewers to do after they watch your videos? These are some of the questions that you should ask yourself the moment the idea of creating content for your channel comes to mind.

Creating your videos haphazardly reflects some level of confusion on your part as a content creator. You want your viewers to know what your channel is all about based on the content you add. This gives the channel some level of authenticity because viewers will see you as an expert in the subject area that you deal with.

The more you talk about a certain topic, the more knowledgeable you appear to be. This increases the likelihood of you gaining more viewers and subscribers. Moreover, it's important to create a situation where people who have viewed your content can confidently refer to others, knowing that you do not create content randomly and aimlessly.

While some goals may be direct, like advertising with the intention of making viewers buy products or services, some may be slightly indirect. Just to trigger your thoughts, here are some of the indirect goals that you might think of:

- collaborating with other content creators on YouTube.

- creating more sources of money via YouTube.

- leaving your nine-to-five job and being a full-time YouTuber.

- making and uploading a certain number of videos within a stipulated time frame.

- exploring other methods of making money on YouTube apart from AdSense.

Please note that goals are broader so they mainly focus on your intended destination. Therefore, you need to put smaller objectives in place. These objectives will give you an idea of how you will achieve the main goal. For instance, if your main goal is to create 22 quality videos during the course of a year, you could decide to produce one each for the first two months, and then two per month for the rest of the year.

Discover Your Audience

When your goals and objectives are in place, you need to know the type of people who you are creating the videos for. Understanding your audience requires a lot of research. When you can clearly define who your customers are, you will find it easier to create content that appeals to them. You will even have a better idea of how best you can present your content. Questions such as "Should I use more visuals in the videos?" are better answered when you know your target audience that much.

Most of the things that you need to know about your audience fall under four main categories:

- **Demographics:** This refers to any statistical properties that define a certain population and the subgroups that are a part of it. Who are the members of your audience based on aspects such as gender, age, income, and geographic location? Such information makes it easier for you to determine the style and approach that works best for them. The language and tone that you should use can also be extrapolated from this.

- **Psychographics:** Psychographics describes a classification model where people are grouped according to aspects such as their attitudes, values, motivation, lifestyle, and aspirations. Such psychological characteristics of your audience allow you to connect with them at a more personal and emotional level. When you understand your audience well, then you can create content that meets their needs and wants. This greatly contributes to the quality of the content that you produce for your viewers.

- **Offline behavior:** Here, you look at the behavior of your audience when they are not on the YouTube channel. Research the audience's employment status, hobbies, buying behavior, and how they generally spend their time. Such information also gives you a better basis for establishing an emotional connection with your audience.

- **Online audience:** How do the people you are targeting behave when they are online? Some of the questions that you should ask for you to get the relevant information are "Which channels do they normally subscribe to?" and "What other social media platforms are they on?" It's also vital to find out how much time they spend on the platforms that they prefer. All this gives you an idea of how your audience interacts with their online environment. As a result, you can also determine how best you can twitch your content to capture their interest.

Knowing your audience before you start creating content for them usually involves a lot of speculation. This is because you don't really know the people that you are targeting at this point. It's only after you have created some content and probably received some feedback that you will have a more solid idea of the characteristics of your potential viewers. Simply put, you will get to know your audience better as time progresses.

If you have already established an audience on other platforms such as LinkedIn, Facebook, and X, you can use these to speculate your prospective audience on YouTube. You can do this by using a poll. Using the X Poll functionality on X is also a great idea.

Find Out More About Competitors

Once you are clear on who your audience is and what they might be expecting from you, keep in mind that there are other YouTubers who are eyeing those same people. These are your competitors. Researching what your competitors are up to helps you to strategize and develop an edge over them. The information that you know about your competitors guides you on the type of content that you should produce if the audience should prefer you over your competitors.

The first step that you should take is to find out who your competitors are. You can do this by scratching for channels that are more likely to be targeting the same audience as you in your niche. Now, take some time to research each of these channels, taking notes on their strengths and weaknesses. Here are some tips on how you can achieve this:

- **Watch their videos:** As you watch the videos of your potential competitors, check out their type of content. Are they long or short videos? How do they generally present their content? This could be in the form of tutorials, pictures, or a combination of text and videos. Take note of any areas of improvement that you could take advantage of.

- **Check video views:** Assess the views for your competitors' videos. This way, you can determine the type of videos that appear to be "crowd pleasers." As a result, you can have a general idea of the videos that can keep people engaged, thereby increasing the chances of developing a loyal audience.

- **Go through the comments:** What are people saying about the videos that your competitors posted? Is there anything that the viewers are asking for, that your competitors have not yet delivered to them? If yes, take note of that and strategize on how you can fulfill the needs of the audience. If there is anything that the viewers are happy with, also be sure to include it so that you maintain buoyancy in the competitive space.

- **Subscribe to the channels of your competitors:** After subscribing to your competitors' channels, assess their patterns for uploading videos. How often do they add new videos?

Going through these steps gives you an idea of the topics that you would like to cover in your channel. You will also identify areas that will allow you to grow a competitive edge in your niche. You then create content that is of better quality.

Plan and Organize Your Content

All the steps that we have discussed so far will give you content ideas for your channel. List down as many ideas as you can think of. Identify the best 10 ideas from the list and embark on creating a publishing calendar. If you want to add content to your channel more often, we recommend that you try weekly schedules. In this case, you will choose your publishing day, say, Tuesday, and then be sure to remain consistent. Doing this is more professional and will keep your audience hooked to your channel.

Planning your schedules also helps you to strategically organize your content in a way that makes it understandable. For example, it becomes easier for you to determine the videos that you can use as end screens on others. You can organize some content into playlists.

Even though you have a plan in place, be sure to leave room for flexibility. Things do change and you should be able to play along, as long the alteration improves your content. For instance, you could come across a piece of news that boosts the quality of your content. You can twitch your schedule accordingly in such cases, though we recommend that you maintain consistency with regard to publishing schedules.

Once you are done organizing your content and planning your schedules, the next step would be to add your content on YouTube. We described steps on how to do this at the beginning of this chapter, in the "Steps for Creating Content on YouTube" section.

Repurposing YouTube Videos

If you want your videos to reach many people, you should think about repurposing them or other social media platforms. One of the advantages of taking this step is that it helps you maintain your existing audience on other platforms and keep them engaged. How best can you repurpose your videos? Consider following these easy steps:

- **Identify the appropriate social media platforms:** Which other platforms do you have an audience that would appreciate the content in your video? You could also research the platforms where your competitors are uploading content. Could it be Facebook, X, TikTok, or LinkedIn? If yes, then go there and post your videos too as this will increase your competitive edge.

- **Analyze the competition on social media:** Find out the type of content that your competitors are posting, as well as the frequency and posting times. Also, find out their engagement rates so that you have an idea of the content that is more appealing to the viewers.

- **Identify opportunities for repurposing:** From your videos, identify content that viewers are more likely to enjoy interacting with, based on the competition analysis that you would have conducted. Remember, you can present the same content in various ways to accommodate the different ways through which people take up information. Video snippets and text-based uploads are some of the ideas that you can consider employing in your repurposing strategy.

Please note that you don't have to put the whole video on your social media platforms. This is because the main idea behind the repurposing strategy is to entice viewers into watching the complete video on YouTube. This partly explains why you should always include a call-to-action that will redirect the audience to the full video on your YouTube channel, thereby increasing your traffic.

Evaluation and Strategy Adjustment

You should track the performance of every video that you add to your channel. We recommend that you do an in-depth check of your videos' progress at least twice a month and you can do this using YouTube Analytics. There are many parameters that you can assess using YouTube Analytics and these include:

- **Impressions:** This refers to the number of times the thumbnails for your video were seen by people, irrespective of whether they clicked them or not.

- **Average view duration:** This metric shows the average length of each view (in minutes), for each video, within a selected date range.

- **Traffic sources:** This describes how the audience ends up viewing your videos. How are they finding them?

- **Watch time:** This is the sum of the time that has been spent by viewers while watching your content.

- **Average percentage viewed:** This describes the average percentage of a selected video that people watch during each view.

- **CTR:** As previously mentioned.

YouTube Content Strategy

A content strategy is a plan where content, be it visual, audio, or written is used to achieve business goals. A content strategy is said to be successful when it is able to have a positive impact on the target audience, even after a purchase has been made. Please note that there are differences between a content strategy and a marketing strategy. Let's differentiate between these two phrases using YouTube as an example.

Generally, a marketing strategy defines the steps that you take in making your channel and content known to your target audience. In other words, the marketing strategy drives traffic to your channel. Once they get there, it's the content strategy that will engage them and turn them into followers, viewers, subscribers, or customers.

Components of a Content Strategy

To further explain what a content strategy is, we will explore its components. Generally, there are four main components that make up a successful content strategy. These are user experience, brand focus, content distribution, and content creation.

Brand Focus

A good content strategy focuses on your brand; that is, what you represent. The topics of your content should remain within the boundaries of your brand. Doing this establishes the consistency that will keep your viewers engaged. Let's suppose that you have a restaurant business that focuses on greens and healthy foods. If you decide to create a YouTube channel for your business, your topics should revolve around the type of food that you make, the ingredients, and why you recommend them as the best option.

Focusing on fuel and transportation prices as a topic in your channel is a slight sway from your brand and purpose. To determine your brand focus, zero in on the common interest between you and your target audience. What both you and your audience care about is what we are basically referring to as your brand focus.

User Experience

In this case, you look at the customer-oriented experience and views with regard to your content. Simply put, your content strategy should address the following questions:

- What attracts your audience into clicking your thumbnails to view your content?

- What will keep them engaged?

- What will make them respond to call-to-actions that encourage them to buy products or services?

- What will encourage them to recommend your channel and brand to others?

In other words, all the people who will visit your channel do have search intentions. To ensure a good user experience, your content should answer the viewers' search queries. They should get what they are looking for.

Content Distribution

While the content on its own is vital, how you distribute it contributes much to audience attraction and engagement. The distribution is explained in terms of the platforms where you publish the work, as well as the timing and timeframes. We recommend that you use different platforms to promote your content and brand. You can use owned media like websites and blogs; earned media like reposts, reviews, and mentions; or paid media like social media ads.

Frequently and consistently uploading videos is a great way of enhancing excellent content distribution. You will need to strike and maintain a balance to ensure that you don't add too many or too few videos. When the uploading frequency is too low, you risk losing audience engagement. If you upload your videos too frequently, your audience may be fatigued such that they might end up missing out on important information.

Content Creation

Brand focus, user experience, and content distribution are all driven by content creation, otherwise, they wouldn't exist. Content creation describes the whole process from coming up with topic ideas to creating your scripts and videos. Though content differs from one channel to the next, the process that you follow in creating it is relatively the same. You will have to:

- come up with ideas that are relevant.

- carry out extensive research to support your ideas.

- create your outlines and scripts.

- create your content and take it through an editing and reviewing process.

- upload your content on YouTube and start promoting it.

Importance of a Content Strategy

Did you know that approximately 45% of marketing professionals find it difficult to create content that is appealing to their target audience? This is the main reason why coming up with a content strategy is crucial. With a well-designed content strategy, you will be clear on the "why" and "how" parts of creating your content. A content strategy keeps you organized so that you maximize engagement with your target audience. Here are some of the problems that you might face when you don't have a content strategy:

- publishing randomly, which might put off your views.

- uploading content that your target audience is less likely to be interested in.

- wrong timing.

Putting a content strategy in place is beneficial to you as a YouTuber in a variety of ways, which include the following:

- You create and distribute your content in a more consistent and organized manner.

- It helps you to gather ideas and themes that are appropriate to the audience that you are targeting.

- It ensures that you deliver quality content at any given time.

- It helps you to create content that aligns with the main goals of your channel.

- It enables you to identify the channels that you can use to distribute your content to the people who need it.

- It is a well-developed plan that keeps plans, tasks, and goals clear to every member of the content creation team.

- It enhances maximum traction, which is part of what you need to make money with YouTube.

Pointers for Developing an Effective Content Strategy

Now, you don't just need a content strategy, but an effective one to get the best results. In this section, we have compiled some tips that will assist you in developing an effective content strategy.

Put a Video SEO Strategy in Place

Remember, when people are searching for certain content on YouTube, there are search words that they use. If your video does not have such words, then the likelihood that your video will appear on the search results and be clicked on is very slim. In essence, that means you will have no business on YouTube. To properly optimize your videos so that they appear at the top of search results, do the following:

- Create titles that are precise but informative. Usually, it's only the first 60 or fewer characters that appear on YouTube, which is why you need to go straight to the point when you create your titles.

- Your video description should have keywords embedded in them. Make sure your characters do not go beyond 70 characters.

- Include proper tags that reflect what your target audience is more likely to be looking for.

- Create high-quality thumbnails that are eye-catching and engaging.

Many people watch YouTube videos using their phones. Therefore, optimize your videos for mobile viewing. Another important thing to note is that a video sitemap helps to provide details about your content to search engines. This is an important step, considering that it helps your videos' ranking.

Be Clear on What Your Video is About

What makes people click on your videos to watch them is the conviction that they are more likely to find what they're looking for. They usually use titles, descriptions, and thumbnails to make the decision of whether to click or not. Remember, you're dealing with people who have busy schedules such that they won't have time to go through a whole video before they realize that the content is not what they were looking for. Therefore, to give potential viewers more information about your video before they watch it:

- **Write a synopsis that is not only accurate but also informative:** Here, you should highlight at least four benefits that your target audience might enjoy. Highlight the main points if the video is a narrative.

- **Transcribe the videos:** This provides the text format of your video content so that the viewers may skim through and decide if they want to watch the actual content.

Make Use of Social Proof

Some reports show that about 50% of customers use customer testimonial videos to make their decisions. This also applies to YouTube content creation and it's what we are referring to as social proof. You can show social proof through likes, views, votes, and comments. Social proof helps you to gain the audience's confidence and support.

Focus on Enhancing Conversions

Once you have succeeded in making people see your video, your focus should be on conversions. You want those people to become viewers, subscribers, and a loyal audience in the long run but this begins with a few steps, which include the following:

- **Calls-to-action:** Be sure to direct the audience to what you want them to do. Your call-to-action should align with what you intend to achieve—whether it's sales, leads, or a dialogue. You can add your call-to-action by adding links or share buttons. You can also use a direct message that tells viewers what to do.

- **Incentives:** Offering immediate incentives increases the chances of clicks from your video. For instance, you can give your viewers discounts once they play your videos. Another example would be to offer a link to a free course to the viewers.

- **Publishing time:** The time when you upload your video contributes much to the conversion rate for your video. You should target a time when your target audience is online so that you maximize getting many views within 48 hours after uploading your video.

- **Creativity:** Videos that showcase creativity are engaging so they keep the audience hooked. Try to make the videos interactive and entertaining. There isn't one way for determining what works best in terms of conversion. You simply have to try different things and see what works best.

- **Length:** Your audience might not go through videos that are too long, especially if they have busy schedules. Of course, this also depends on the type of content that you are streaming.

Other Steps

The steps that are outlined here have been discussed in depth earlier. These are:

- selecting the right distribution channels for your content.

- marketing and promoting your videos.

- evaluating the performance of your videos.

In this chapter, we discussed how you can improve the quality of your videos. We highlighted the importance of coming up with a content strategy in a bid to create videos of better quality. Once you have good quality content, you need to identify and implement ways to grow your subscribers, and this will be covered in the next chapter.

Checklist

The first checklist is for the steps that you should follow when creating your content on YouTube. The second one highlights how you can create good content on YouTube. Finally, we have created another checklist that will help you make sure your content strategy is effective enough to promote conversions.

The checklist for the steps that you should take in creating your YouTube content is presented below.

	Ensure that you create eyecatching titles, thumbnails, video outlines and scripts.
	Editing and review your videos before publishing.

	Create goals for your channel.
	Discover your audience.
	Consistently analyse the competition.
	Plan your content and repurpose your videos.
	Evaluate and adjust your strategy if needed.
	Plan your SEO strategy.
	Choose the right distribution channels for your content.
	Market and promote your content.

Chapter 4:

Strategies for Growing Subscribers

One of the most important metrics in assessing the success of your YouTube channel over time is by checking the number of subscribers. The more subscribers you have, the greater the indication that you are producing content that is relevant to a particular audience. YouTube regards a quick rise in the number of subscribers as a sign that your content has various characteristics that relate well to the target audience.

This puts you in a better position to monetize the videos on your YouTube channel. In this chapter, we will explore various ways through which you can gain more subscribers for your channel. We will also discuss how you can use the YouTube algorithm to your advantage so that you can reach different levels on YouTube.

Gain More Subscribers on YouTube

Of course, the first step for you to start getting subscribers on your channel is adding some videos. However, this could be a small part of the whole process of growing your subscriber capital. There are many other things that you can do to increase traffic to your channel and also turn views into substantial subscriptions.

You will also notice that most of the tips that we will highlight with regard to growing your subscriber base also apply in retaining the ones you already have. Once you are able to retain the subscribers that you have already attained, you can continue working on attracting more viewers. Let's see what you can do to gain more subscribers on YouTube.

Power Playlists

Power playlists work in a similar way to regular playlists, though they yield better results. Generally, other playlists are organized based on topics. For example, you can have a playlist of "cooking videos" or "vegetable gardening videos." Power playlists are created based on outcomes. For instance, "How to lose extra pounds and become slender" is a power playlist. "How to become a millionaire from scratch" is another good example of a power playlist. In both examples, there is more emphasis on the outcome, and this is what will attract the target audience into subscribing to the channel.

The "More on That Soon" Strategy

Ideally, people subscribe after viewing your content. This is a sign that they are hooked by your previous content and so they anticipate more quality videos from you. Therefore, you should take advantage of that curiosity and tease them with a bit of what you will discuss in your next video. Leave them a little hanging and tell them to expect more information in the next streaming. When you use this strategy, it is important for you to live up to your promise so that you keep the viewers engaged, while nurturing their trust as well.

Content That Is Informative and Engaging

The content of your videos should be informative and engaging enough to keep the viewers glued to our channel. The more they spend time on your channel, the greater the probability that they will subscribe to the channel. Here are some quick tips that can assist you to create content that is engaging enough to attract and retain subscribers:

- Create content that targets a specific audience.

- Include visuals in your content as this makes it more appealing.

- Pattern interrupts, cards, and end-screens keep your viewers engaged.

- Include examples where necessary. They help the viewer to relate to what you're talking about.

- Always begin your videos with hooks or anecdotes that will trigger the viewer's interest to watch the rest of the video.

Brand Watermarks

Brand watermarks allow your audience to subscribe to your channel inside your video. Some YouTubers reported that using fancy and unique band watermarks may attract little if any subscriptions because viewers tend to ignore them. This could be because they might just appear like some creative icons that are part of the videos, not necessarily buttons for subscribing.

Adding a brand watermark that is similar to the normal "subscribe button" that is used by YouTube could help to rectify this issue. Brian Dean tried this strategy and realized a 70% increase in the number of subscribers compared to the time when he used a more creative and customized one.

Publish Videos More Frequently

Would you want to subscribe to a channel where videos are uploaded once in a blue moon? Certainly not and this is the reason why your viewers are less likely to subscribe to your videos if you take too long before adding another one. Uploading videos to your channel more frequently keeps your target audience engaged.

It's a great way to keep them in the loop and allow them to remain in touch with the flow from one video to the next. Adding videos more frequently retains viewers on your channel. The more time they spend on your channel, the greater the chances that they will subscribe.

One study showed that YouTubers who publish videos at least once a week tend to perform better than those who take longer. More frequent publishing gives a better boost to your subscriber base when you do it consistently and when the videos that you add are informative and original.

Remind Viewers to Subscribe

You might have noticed that not all viewers are turned into subscribers in channels. However, this doesn't mean that the viewers who didn't subscribe do not like the content on your channel. They might even continue to visit the channel often but without subscribing. You just have to remind such people to subscribe, and they will surely do. You can do this strategically so that it doesn't look like all you care about is subscriptions. For instance, you can ask the viewers to subscribe when you add new content to your channel.

Build and Nurture a Relationship With Your Community

You don't want to be the type of YouTuber who only focuses on adding one video after another, without engaging your audience. Content creators who make efforts to form relationships with their audience gain their trust, thereby increasing the chances of earning more subscriptions. You can interact with your community by responding to their comments in a professional and respectful way.

If they make comments that are not quite appealing to you, try to reflect calmness in your response and explain yourself if there is a need to. Thank your audience for their comments as this can even attract more with free content ideas that can take the quality of your work to another level.

Follow back your audience on their own social media platforms to make your relationship more solid. You can also consider partnering with other peers who are also content creators on YouTube and promoting each other by subscribing to each other's channels.

Channel Branding

Effective channel branding tells the audience about what your channel is all about, thereby narrowing down what they should expect when they visit. The banner on your channel is one of the vital baits that turn views into subscriptions. This banner tells the viewers about your brand, and it should give them solid reasons why they should stay glued to your channel. Ideally, your banner should be neat, compelling, and strongly represent your brand.

Your channel icon, which is also called the logo, could be the one to attract potential viewers. Your logo is "you" so it should clearly represent your brand. Just by having a logo, your work appears more professional and that can be what it takes to attract the attention of subscribers.

Another unique way of branding your channel is by customizing the URL. This allows your brand to feature in the URL. To customize the URL for your channel, go to YouTube Studio and select "Customization" in the menu on the left. Select "Basic Info" and then "Channel URL." Please note that you are required to have at least 100 subscribers to your channel before you can customize your URL.

The Quality of Your Videos

A more frequent schedule for publishing your videos is a great idea, but not when the quality of the content is being compromised in the process. Combining the quantity and quality metrics will see you gain more subscribers. Our viewers know what they are looking for when they visit your channel and if they are unable to get it, they will simply disappear without hitting the "subscribe" button. Embrace quality so that you meet the needs of your potential viewers, and you won't have to beg for subscriptions from your audience.

Promote Your Videos

Promoting your videos beyond the YouTube platform is another lucrative strategy for growing your loyal audience. When you repurpose your videos and present the information in other formats and on other platforms such as Facebook, the viewers become enticed to watch the full videos on YouTube. This drives traffic to your channel. Remember, the more views, the greater the possibility of getting more subscriptions. You can promote your content by:

- adding your content to social media platforms like X, Facebook, and LinkedIn.

- incorporating links for collaborating with authoritative websites and other fellow YouTubers.

- participating in blog discussions and relevant forums.

- using email marketing. (In this case, you simply have to incorporate the link or your channel into your signature.)

Custom Channel Trailers

The customization settings on YouTube provide the functionality that makes it possible for you to stream certain content to subscribers and not non-subscribers and vice-versa. You can take advantage of this option and create a channel trailer that is directed at non-subscribers. This trailer gives these unsubscribed viewers more information that enlightens them on what to expect from your channel. Provide them with convincing information that highlights why they should subscribe.

Incorporate Your Videos in Blogs

When you create your blog posts, consider incorporating links to your YouTube videos. This is one of the strategies that are less explored, yet it is a good source of viewers who can turn into subscribers. This is because people who take their time to read your blog posts already show interest in your content. If they see links to the video that is linked to the information, they are more likely to click on it.

Moreover, many people would prefer listening to an audio or watching a video that gives them the information that they need than reading through the text. Therefore, embedding video links for your YouTube content will appear as a great bonus to such people. On the other hand, you will be driving traffic to your videos, thereby elevating the probability of them being subscribed to.

When you add videos to your blog post, be sure to do it strategically so that it appears necessary. Don't make it look like you're forcing the video onto the blog post. For instance, you can add a video so that it elaborates more on a certain point that you mentioned in the post. You can also add your videos so that they provide steps for a certain procedure or tip that you emphasized in your blog post.

Optimize Your Videos

We explained how to optimize your videos and channel earlier in this book. Therefore, we will not go into detail here. When you use exact keywords in the title of your video, it's more likely to rank higher. This comes with more views and hence, more probable subscriptions.

Adding timestamps and links to your description also puts your videos in a better position to get views and subscriptions. Timestamps make it easier for your viewers to skip parts of your videos and go straight to the sections that are more interesting to them. Such convenience may attract subscriptions.

Incorporating links to your other videos keeps your viewers connected to your content, thereby maintaining engagement. Video tags make it easier for potential viewers to search for and find your video. Such an increased possibility of contact between the target audience and your videos might turn into subscriptions to your videos and channel.

Use Subscriber Magnets

Subscriber magnets are videos that generate more subscribers compared to others. Therefore, by funneling the channel visitors to "subscriber magnets," the graph for subscribers will more likely grow. Getting this done only involves a few simple steps, as follows:

1. Go to YouTube Analytics and select "Subscribers," prior to clicking "See more."

2. Identify the video that attracted more subscriptions than the others in the previous month. This is your subscriber magnet.

3. Promote this video and let it reach as many people as possible.

Showcasing Your Content

How you showcase your content on your channel plays a role in enticing viewers into subscribing. You could present your videos in such a way that the best ones are at the front so that they are the first to be seen by your audience. These are your bait for making viewers consider subscribing.

A Channel Tagline

The channel tagline refers to the characteristics that are unique to that particular channel. It describes those things that could make your videos stand out from thousands of other similar content that is available on YouTube. The channel tagline positions your videos, making them excel and gain a competitive edge that gives them popularity among your viewers. If this happens, it is a sign of a possible increase in the number of subscriptions.

You can create a simple tagline for your channel in just a few steps:

1. **Identify the unique point for your channel:** You can think of this as your main selling point. Could it be that you have a different way of doing exercise? Maybe, you have a unique ingredient that you use in making certain dishes. As long as it's something that is not identified with other channels, then you are good to go.

2. **Include the tagline in your channel art:** The point that you identified in (1) above is your tagline. Add this tagline to your channel art and make sure that it has a large font so that it stands out.

3. **Include tagline in the channel trailer:** Doing this emphasizes the tagline, thereby making it known to the people who visit your channel.

Long Videos

Yes, it's true that people tend to click on shorter videos because they just want to quickly get what they are looking for. However, one study that analyzed various factors that help videos to rank at the top of the list in YouTube search results discovered that longer videos are better. Interesting, isn't it?

Therefore, create longer videos that rank higher on the YouTube search engine. This way, you increase contact between your videos and the target audience. In turn, the likelihood of people subscribing to your videos increases. Videos that rank lower are rarely clicked on so getting more subscribers becomes difficult.

Link Certain Subscriptions to Incentives

Naturally, people are attracted to benefits, no matter how small they might appear to be. When you make offers that can only be accessed by people who would have subscribed to your channel, you indirectly encourage viewers to become subscribers. Offering incentives that target the audience that already views your content is the easiest way to go.

This is because by continuously viewing your content, these people might be showing interest in your videos. For example, you can offer a giveaway that is only available to subscribers. You could offer a brush set if your channel focuses on makeup, for example. Be sure to live up to your promises as this also counts when it comes to earning subscriptions.

"Hearting" the Viewers' Comments

You can respond to good comments and compliments by the viewers just by adding a heart. This is what we are referring to as hearting (or liking a comment). Doing this makes it easy for you to highlight outstanding comments for your audience. Each time you give a hearting response to a comment on your channel, the viewer receives a notification.

Here are the findings that were reported by YouTube: "We've found that viewers who have received a heart on their comment are three times more likely to click on the notification (than with other types of notifications), potentially leading more viewers back to your channel". This means that heart notifications can earn you up to 300% more clicks than other notifications. This brings the viewers back to your channel and the more they linger around, the greater the likelihood that they will subscribe.

Optimizing for Your Videos' Watch Time

YouTube promotes videos that are watched more by its audience. Such videos have higher chances of being in the spotlight where viewers can easily see them, and possibly subscribe. Most of the videos that you see on YouTube's homepage have content that is highly watched. This information shows that maximizing the watch time on your videos is of paramount importance. Pattern interrupts are one of the most effective methods for making viewers watch your videos for longer.

Pattern interrupts are events or actions that alter the thought patterns of an individual. They make your videos unique, in addition to triggering the curiosity that will keep your viewers glued to see and hear more. Include corny jokes and graphics to give your videos that unique touch that will make them captivating and engaging.

Using the Social Media Preview

One of the things that most people overlook when they post their YouTube videos on other social media platforms is that those platforms also want to retain their viewers because that is the only way they remain in business. They don't want their audience to be going to YouTube. As a result, these social media platforms do not promote videos that:

- are not native.

- will direct their viewers to YouTube.

Therefore, use these two pointers to strategically share your content on other social media platforms while also maximizing driving traffic to your YouTube channel. You can use the social media preview, which allows you to get many views, some of which will make an extra step to watch your videos on YouTube as well. Here are the steps that will help you achieve this:

1. Get a video clip from the recent YouTube video that you want to promote. Make sure it's short—ideally, not more than 90 seconds in length. Also, make sure that your clip is not selling out your full video. It should present just one idea so that it triggers the curiosity to watch the rest of the video.

2. Add the clip as a native video on the social media platform of your choice. Simply put, don't add it as a YouTube video. This is vital, considering that native posts receive more views. There is data that shows that video posts that are native to Facebook have 10 times better chances of being shared than those that are directly linked to YouTube.

3. Add the link to your full YouTube video as the first comment to the native video post that you created. Viewers who are interested in more information will easily click on the link. Such people could subscribe to your full video once they get to the YouTube platform.

The YouTube Algorithm

The YouTube algorithm refers to a recommendation system that YouTube uses to streamline suggestions for videos that should be watched by the identified platform's users. In other words, even though there are many videos that are published on YouTube, not all of them are suggested to over a billion users on the platform. The YouTube algorithm recommends some videos, thereby positioning them for increased views and subscriptions.

The YouTube algorithm operates through any of the following three discovery and selection systems:

- The one that identifies and selects videos that are shown on YouTube's homepage.

- The one that suggests videos that viewers should watch next.

- The one that decides the ranking of the results when visitors on YouTube type their search words or phrases.

How It Works

Please note that the YouTube algorithm's goal is two-way. First, the algorithm is meant to identify the video that answers the search query of each viewer. Second, the algorithm intends to keep the viewers watching YouTube content. These two pointers contribute to how the algorithm selects videos that are watched by YouTube's audience.

Over the years, there have been changes or improvements in the way the YouTube algorithm works. For example, there was a point where the algorithm depended on the click that people made on videos as they sought specific content. The challenge that came with this was that content creators began to use clickbait to attract people to click and view their content. The result of such a scenario could be predicted—the satisfaction of the viewers was compromised. Well, that was then, how does the algorithm currently work?

How Does YouTube Determine Its Homepage Algorithm?

Each time you get on YouTube, you will be welcomed by a page that shows various videos that the platform's algorithm thinks are interesting to you. This page that you see first is the homepage. Usually, the selection that you find on the homepage is more general because the algorithm wouldn't have figured out what you really want. This is the same experience that your viewers go through when they open YouTube. Videos that appear on the homepage are selected based on the following:

- **Performance:** Metrics such as average view duration, likes, dislikes, CTR, and the average percentage viewed are the ones that are used in determining the performance of your videos. Generally, when you publish a video on YouTube, it will appear on the homepages of a few people. Its performance at this point is what will determine if the video will be shown to more people. In other words, the video should get more clicks, views, likes, and other positive metrics for it to be recommended on homepages for more people.

- **Personalization:** If a viewer has been using YouTube for some time, the algorithm can use their watch and search history to determine what they are more likely to watch. If there is a certain type of content that the viewer tends to watch more often, similar videos will appear more often on the YouTube homepage on their gadget. As interest changes, the algorithm picks this up and alters the content that appears on the homepage.

How Does YouTube Determine Its Suggested Videos Algorithm?

When people are watching videos on YouTube, there is usually another stand-by one that is suggested for them to watch next. Here is how this works: When one visits YouTube and watches a few videos, the algorithm will pick up the interests of the viewers at the moment. It will then use that information to suggest more videos that the viewer might find interesting. These suggested videos are shown on the right side of the screen.

Performance and personalization are considered in identifying the videos that are more appealing to the viewer. In addition to these, YouTube also uses the following pointers:

- It can show videos that have topics that are related to what the viewer has been watching.

- It can show videos that are usually watched together by other viewers.

- It can suggest videos that have been previously watched by the viewer.

YouTube is a video streaming platform, but it has the functionality to allow viewers to use it as a search engine. This means that viewers can insert their search queries and videos that better match their text will pop up. This also implies that as a content creator on YouTube, you should be well-versed in how SEOs work so that they can optimize your videos accordingly.

Let's go through the important aspects that determine whether your videos will appear among the search results or not:

- **Keywords:** If the keywords on your video match those that would have been inserted by the viewers in YouTube's search engine, then it might appear among the reach results. The extent to which the keywords match also determines whether your video will appear at the top of the list or not. Ideally, appearing at the top of the list is better because your videos are more likely to be clicked on. If you want your videos to appear when viewers search for "cataract treatment," then you should include these words in your video.

- **Performance:** If your videos appear in search results, metrics such as CTRs and likes begin to matter. In the event that viewers find your videos appealing, then they are more likely to spend more time watching them. If this happens, the videos will be shown again when people use keywords to search for content.

How to Use the YouTube Algorithm to Your Advantage

Did you know that approximately 81% of YouTube users in America watch videos that are suggested to them by the algorithm? Also, there is a general consensus that for every individual, 70% of their time on YouTube is spent watching videos that are suggested by the algorithm. Understanding what the YouTube algorithm is all about is good, but having a solid idea of how it can work for you is better because then you can increase the chances of your videos being watched.

This section will assist you to achieve the latter. However, before we delve into the nitty-gritty of how you can use the YouTube algorithm to your advantage, we will highlight some of the key areas that are considered by algorithms as far as viewers are concerned. Knowing these areas helps you to identify what you can change, emphasize, improve, add, or remove from your videos as a way of increasing their chances of being watched by potential viewers. These are:

- **Likes and dislikes:** The algorithm checks the use of "like" and "dislike" buttons by the viewers.

- **Content being watched:** What type of videos are being watched by the viewers?

- **Content that is not watched:** The algorithm assesses videos that are not watched by viewers. Even those that are clicked but not watched are included in this category.

- **Past searches:** The keywords that the viewers might have been using to search for the videos that they like are also important. If you can incorporate such keywords in your published content, then your videos are more likely to appear after searches in YouTube's search engine.

- **Impressions:** When YouTube's algorithm suggests your videos to viewers, how often do they click and watch them? This matters much because more impressions are associated with better results.

- **Geography and demographic information:** Videos can be suggested to viewers based on their locations and demographic parameters.

- **How old the video is:** How long your video has been available online also matters much. Usually, the YouTube algorithm suggests newer videos to the **audience.**

- **Feedback related to the "not interested" option:** If there are many viewers who click the "not interested" option on your videos, this might negatively affect the chances of your videos being suggested to the potential audience.

- **Thumbnails for your videos:** Are your video thumbnails authentic and representative of the content in your videos? Viewers respond negatively to misleading and unattractive thumbnails.

- **Engagement:** Aspects such as shares, likes, and comments are a sign that people are interested in the content of your videos. As a result, the algorithm will suggest it to more of the YouTube audience.

- **Uploading frequency on the channel:** The more you upload content the more frequently, the YouTube algorithm will pick that up and recommend your videos. This is because the channel will be regarded as active by the algorithm.

- **Speed of popularity:** Videos that earn popularity at a higher rate have a higher probability of making it to the Trending page.

Now that you have an idea of the things that the YouTube algorithm looks at, you can strategize so that your videos have better chances of being suggested to the audience. Let's go through some of the tips that make it possible for you to achieve this goal.

Avoid Using Clickbait

Clickbait are titles or thumbnails that are misleading as they are only meant to attract clicks on a video. They, sometimes, increase traffic to your videos and the CTR gets higher. However, it usually doesn't take much time before the viewers realize that they have been tricked. As a result, they won't watch the videos. They even leave bad comments that shun other potential viewers away.

It is important to note that various components that are considered by the YouTube algorithm tend to work together in making your videos appear in searches. This means that only focusing on the CTR is not such a great idea because you then neglect other vital factors such as increasing the watch time and engagement of the viewers.

We, therefore, recommend that you create awesome titles and thumbnails that are authentic and related to the content that you present in your videos. This way, you raise the chances of earning more likes, shares, and positive comments. This will increase the traffic to your videos, while also increasing the watch time of the visitors to your channel. More importantly, the YouTube algorithm is more likely to recommend your videos to even more users.

Create Great and Authentic Thumbnails

Together with your titles, thumbnails are usually the first thing that people see with regard to your video. They help the viewers decide whether to click and possibly watch your video or not.

As you create your thumbnails, always remember that humans are social beings, so they are naturally attracted to other people. This notion is further supported by a Netflix study that highlighted that faces that reflect certain emotions, whether good or bad, have the best likelihood of attracting viewers and even keeping them engaged. Therefore, using thumbnails that have faces that show emotions may attract viewers into watching your video. For example, if the video will aid relief in physical pain, you could show the transition from the sadness caused by the pain to the joy when the pain is gone.

You can also use text in your thumbnails but do so sparingly. The text on your thumbnail is another opportunity to use keywords that are associated with your video, thereby increasing the probability that it will appear in response to YouTube. Don't explain too much—the title will do that job.

Remember to include your logo on your thumbnail. Some viewers who already love your videos are more likely to click without thinking, just by seeing that it is your brand video, on the thumbnail.

Content Consistency Matters

Make it easier for the algorithm to identify your videos by sticking to your brand niche. As time progresses, you might notice that you will get a lot of interesting ideas, some of which are too broad and a little off from the goals of your channel. Be careful of these and do everything possible to narrow down your brand niche.

If your channel was meant to provide cooking recipes, stick to that and avoid the urge to start exploring weight-loss exercises and other unrelated topics. Remain consistent so that you maintain customer engagement. The YouTube algorithm will identify your videos and recommend them to more viewers.

Create a Good Description

Never underrate the power of your video description. It's not always the case that the titles and thumbnails give viewers all the information that they need to decide whether to watch your video or not. At times, they need a little extra information that will help them confirm that your video contains what they are looking for before watching for a few minutes. Therefore, you should craft a video description that is not only valuable but also SEO-focused so that its intentions are clear to the YouTube algorithm.

To do so, you should embark on research so that you find out the keywords that your potential viewers are more likely to use when they search for videos that provide similar content to yours. List them and then incorporate them into your video description and ensure a natural flow of the sentences. When your target audience does their searches on YouTube, your video will be in a better position to be suggested to them by the algorithm.

Publish According to a Defined Schedule

The YouTube algorithm does not only look at the number of videos that you have already published but also the frequency at which you do so. So, consistency is also vital with regard to publishing your videos just as it is when it comes to the content. Keep track of your publishing schedule to ensure such consistency. Just by doing this, you will be giving your videos a competitive edge and better recognition by the YouTube algorithm.

Strategize and ensure that your audience is engaged with your videos. Do everything possible to make them watch your videos for longer. Also, target increasing the general watch time for your videos. You can do this by encouraging those who see your videos to share them with their connections. The traffic to your videos increases—so does the watch time. Another noble strategy is to refer your viewers to your other videos. This way, you will have the same viewers watching more of your videos. The YouTube algorithm will take note of that and "promote" your videos.

Engage as the Content Creator

Apart from having your viewers engage, the algorithm also notices when you also do something to connect with your audience. Responding to the viewers' comments is one of the best ways to engage, even though simply "liking" the posts also works. Your audience will appreciate that, and this will retain them on your channel, while they connect with your brand even more. The YouTube algorithm will notice all that.

The YouTube Creator Awards

YouTube rewards content creators based on the number of subscribers on their channels. To this, the platform has creator benefit levels that accommodate all creators from the one with one subscriber. Each level is associated with various features. As the levels increase, the creators are given more access to YouTube Space studios. In this section, we will highlight the various content creator levels that you should look forward to on YouTube.

- **Silver Creator Award:** First, there is the silver creator award, which includes content creators who have at least 100,000 subscribers. Once you get to this stage, you have the leverage to apply for a digital verification badge.

- **Gold Creator Award:** Once you reach or go beyond 1,000,000 subscribers.

- **Diamond Creator Award**: You only get this award when your subscriber count reaches or exceeds 10 million.

- **Custom Creator Award:** Previously, this was the award that was given to channels that would have exceeded 50 million subscribers. As of 2021, this award is now granted based on YouTube's discretion.

- **Red Diamond Creator Award:** This is for channels whose number of subscribers is equal to or greater than 100 million.

- Accumulating as many subscribers as possible is of paramount importance for the growth of your channel and the ultimate goal of monetization. This chapter opened your eyes to many ideas that can help you to attract more viewers and turn watch time into subscriptions. In the next chapter, we will delve deeper into how best you can engage with your audience.

Checklist

Assess your progress with regard to strategies for gaining more subscribers over time using points in the table below.

	Use brand watermarks.
	Optimize your videos.
	Use subscriber magnets.
	Brand your channels.
	Create longer videos.

	Use channel taglines.
	Comment or react to viewer comments.
	Use social media previews.
	Incentivize subscriptions.
	Publish more frequently if possible.
	Update your thumbnails to be attractive and authentic.
	Create good descriptions.

Chapter 5:

Audience Engagement

Audience engagement on YouTube is a summary of how viewers interact with your channel or videos. They are usually presented in the form of metrics such as likes, subscriptions, dislikes, views, and comments. The overall engagement of the target audience is a reflection of the popularity of your videos. In the previous chapter, we also emphasized that the YouTube algorithm also considers audience engagement when it suggests videos to visitors on the platform.

This means that the more engagement you have from viewers, the greater the likelihood of your videos even reaching more eyes. Moreover, videos that are associated with greater audience interaction are better positioned to earn more subscriptions, thereby possibly accessing more benefits and functionalities on YouTube.

The dream of monetizing your YouTube channel will come true when viewers engage more. This is because engagement is generally a sign that the target audience loves your content and finds it relevant. In this chapter, we will explore various aspects of audience engagement. By the time you get to the end of the chapter, you should be able to analyze your YouTube Analytics so that you can strategically move toward learning more about your audience, thereby further growing your YouTube channel.

YouTube Analytics

The fact that there is forced competition on the YouTube platform cannot be overstated. For you to stand a chance of being a successful YouTuber, you have to somehow have the YouTube algorithm on your side. Therefore, you cannot afford to ignore anything that can assist you to optimize your videos so that they are highly recognized by the algorithm. Using YouTube Analytics is one such endeavor.

YouTube Analytics will help you to have an idea of the extent to which your target audience is engaging with your published content. Such information will then enlighten you on what you should do to improve the way target viewers interact with your videos as this is important if you are to make money using YouTube.

The audience engagement that you note using YouTube Analytics gives you an idea with regard to the type of content that is more appealing to the target audience. You will know whether they are more interested in vlogs, tutorials, or how-tos, among other options. In this section, we will discuss how you can access YouTube Analytics, as well as how to use it to assess viewer engagement and other important aspects that will, in one way or the other, affect how people interact with your published content.

Accessing YouTube Analytics

The way you can access YouTube Analytics differs, depending on the type of gadget that you are using. Check the steps that are applicable to you in this section and start using YouTube Analytics.

Using a Computer?

If you are using a computer, follow these steps:

1. Use relevant details to sign into YouTube Studio at *studio.youtube.com*. Alternatively, go to your YouTube account and click on the **icon** for your profile. Choose "**YouTube Studio**" from the options that come up.

2. Once you are on YouTube Studio, go through the menu on your left-hand side and click on "**Analytics.**" This will land you on the YouTube Analytics page.

These steps that we highlighted above will give you analytics at the channel level. Please note that it is also possible for you to analyze your data at the video level through the steps that are listed below:

1. Open "**YouTube Studio**" as highlighted earlier.

2. Go to "**Content**," which is found on the menu on your left side.

3. Point to the video that you want to assess and choose "**Analytics**."

Another point to note—if you want more expanded reports that give you more detail, simply click on "**See More**" or "**Advanced Mode**."

Using Your Android Phone, iPad, or iPhone?

If you are using your Android phone, you can access YouTube Analytics in two ways. You can access it via the YouTube Android app or the YouTube Studio app for Android. Let's go through the actual steps together.

If you are using the YouTube Android app:

1. Go to your **YouTube app**.

2. Click on your **profile picture** and then go to "**Your Channel**."

3. Select "**Analytics**" from the middle menu.

If you are using the YouTube Studio app for Android:

1. Go to your **YouTube Studio** app.

2. Select "**Analytics**" from the bottom menu.

Let's suppose that you want to see reports from the video level, follow these steps:

1. Go to your **YouTube Studio** app.

2. Choose "**Content**" from the bottom menu.

3. Identify the video that you want to analyze, click on it, go to the Analytics section, and then select "**View More**."

More on YouTube Analytics Tabs

Once you get to YouTube Analytics, you will see many tabs. Some of the information under these tabs will give you metrics that are directly related to audience engagement. In some instances, you have to extrapolate. This section will take you through the various information that you can derive from YouTube Analytics.

The Overview Tab

Under the "Overview" tab, you will get a summary of the overall performance of your videos and channel. Metrics such as watch time, views, and subscribers will be highlighted. If you are in the YPP, your estimated revenue will also be shown. Other reports that you will find on this tab will be for:

- **Typical performance:** This is a comparison of either a video's or channel's typical performance. Generally, the channel or video is doing well when positive audience engagement is higher.

- **Realtime:** This report shows how you are performing over 1 hour of 48 hours. Such information enlightens you on the current performance of your channel or video.

- **Your top content in this period:** Here, your videos are ranked based on the number of views that they have over a period of the previous four weeks.

The Content Tab

The "Content" tab is on a channel level, and it provides you with information on how potential viewers find your videos and how they engage with your published content. Simply put, the Content tab will give you access to reach and engagement reports that you can find in the All, Live, Videos, Posts, and Shorts categories. Here are some of the metrics that you should expect to find:

- **Views:** The sum of authentic views on your published content for live streams, videos, and shorts. This is an important metric for evaluating audience engagement.

- **Published content:** This highlights all the videos, live streams, posts, and Shorts that are already published and available to viewers.

- **Subscribers:** You certainly want to know how many people have subscribed to your channel as this also enlightens you on viewer engagement.

- **Impressions:** Here, you see information on how many times your thumbnail was seen by the YouTube audience. You will also see if there were any views that resulted from the impressions. Not only that, but you will also see how the views turned to watch time.

- **Key moments for audience retention:** Interestingly, you can also see the extent to which different moments in your videos captured the attention of the viewers. The "typical retention" functionality also allows you to compare 10 of your latest videos, as long as they are similar in length.

- **Top videos:** Here, you can see your most popular videos. In other words, you can see the videos that have the greatest audience engagement.

The Reach Tab

Through the Reach tab, you can determine how your target audience comes across your channel. Some of the metrics that you will access under this tab are impressions, CTRs, and views. You will also see unique viewers, in addition to the following reports:

- **Traffic source types:** This highlights how viewers discovered your content. Through this metric, you can determine the contact points that are giving you more views so that you can maximize them.

- **YouTube search:** This describes the search-term traffic that drove the YouTube audience to your videos. This further helps you to know the keywords that are incorporated in your videos, in a bid to enhance audience engagement.

- **Bell notifications sent:** This refers to the sum of bell notifications that are sent to subscribers to let them know of the new things happening on your channel. Subscribers who receive such notifications would have highlighted their interest in getting them and that's a form of engagement on their part.

- **Playlists:** Here, you see the views from the most-watched playlists where your videos are also part of the list.

- **External:** This report shows the traffic from other websites, platforms, or apps where your link was embedded.

- **Impressions and how they led to watch time:** This shows the transition from the number of times your video thumbnails appeared to viewers, to the CTR, and ultimately, watch time.

The Engagement Tab

Under the "Engagement" tab, you will get highlights on the amount of time that viewers spend watching your content. The two most important metrics, in this case, are average view duration and watch time. Here at other reports that you will see under the "Engagement" tab:

- **Likes versus dislikes:** This helps you quickly have an idea of the audience's feelings toward your published video. More likes are a sign of positive engagement, and they could turn into subscriptions and loyal viewing.

- **Top tagged products:** If the products that you tagged in your video attract and receive the best audience engagement, they will be shown in this report.

- **Audience retention:** This report shows the extent to which the viewers' attention is captured by certain different moments of your video.

- **End screen element click rate:** This shows how many times the end screen element was clicked on by viewers.

The Audience Tab

If you are wondering what type of viewers are watching your videos, go to the "Audience" tab. Under this tab, the viewers will be categorized into new and returning viewers. You will also see unique viewers and those who subscribed to your channel or videos. The total number of all viewers is also stated.

You can also check the following reports under the Audience tab:

- **Age and gender:** YouTube Analytics uses the information of all the people who would have signed into your channel, regardless of the devices that they use, to determine the ages and gender of your viewers.

- **When your viewers are on YouTube:** Based on activity within the last four weeks, the online patterns of the viewers on your channel and YouTube as a whole, are established.

- **Top geographies:** This report will classify the viewers based on their geographical locations. This information is gathered through IP addresses.

- **Videos growing your audience:** This report tells you the number of new viewers on your channel over the last consecutive 90 days. To create this data, the online patterns of the viewers on your channel are monitored.

- **Watch time from subscribers:** Here, you find the watch time that is related to subscribers.

- **Top subtitle/closed caption (CC) languages:** What are the subtitled languages of your viewers? This is the question that is answered by this report, and it's derived from the use of subtitles/CC.

- **Channels your audience watches:** Here, you can see the other channels that your viewers watch on YouTube. This information is gathered based on the viewers' online activity over the last consecutive 28 days, irrespective of the devices that they use.

- **Subscriber bell notifications:** This report gives you statistics on the number of subscribers to whom bell notifications are sent. It is also possible for you to see the sum of the subscribers who actually receive the bell notifications.

- **Content your audience watches:** Here, information is gathered based on the viewers' online activity over the past seven days. The report shows the content that your audience often watches apart from that on your channel. Depending on the amount of data available, it is possible to filter the data by Shorts, Videos, and Live.

The Research Tab

This tab answers the question, "What is being searched for by my audience throughout the YouTube platform?" To get that information, YouTube Analytics gives you reports on:

- **Searches across YouTube:** The search topics that you explored the most are reflected here. You will also see those of your viewers and audience. Please note that the information is based on recorded activity over the last consecutive 28 days.

- **Your viewer's searches:** This report shows the search words and phrases that are used by your viewers and audience in YouTube's search engines. You will also search terms that are used by the audience for channels that are similar to yours. The volume of the viewers is also shown so that you can assess which search words are used more than the others. Please note that the presented information is based on activity over the past 28 days.

The Revenue Tab

Yes, the "Revenue" tab focuses more on your earnings and that is if you are in the YPP. However, some of the metrics that are presented under this tab can give you an idea of the audience engagement that is associated with some videos. For instance, the report on "top-earning videos" will show you the videos that most probably had the most overall engagement over a certain period. Other reports that you will find under the Revenue tab are:

- Revenue sources

- Ad types

- Transaction revenue

- Monthly estimated revenue

Based on the information that you learned from this section, we can safely say that YouTube Analytics is a good companion when it comes to evaluating audience engagement on your channel. It will enable you to identify areas of improvement with regard to audience engagement. For example, if there are relevant search terms that the audience to channels that are similar to yours are using, why not try them as well?

You could boost the contact chances between your videos and the people who will appreciate them. If the links that you might have embedded on your Facebook posts are yielding more traffic to your channel, leading to higher audience engagement, then why not explore that strategy even more? If "how to" videos seem to be attracting more engagement than the tutorials, then there is no harm in putting more effort into the former.

You simply have to maintain an open mindset as you go through the reports on YouTube Analytics. This will assist you to explore strategies that you probably thought would never work and that could be your breakthrough to better audience engagement.

Subscriber Count vs. Audience Engagement Rate

One of the assumptions that many people make, probably including yourself, is that the greater the number of subscribers, the higher the engagement rate. We are not outruling the fact that this can be so, but it is just not always the case. Not to worry—we will explain what this means in this section. We will look at how subscriber counts affect the YouTube engagement rate of micro- and macro-influencers.

Macro-Influencers and Engagement Rate

Macro-influencers are content creators whose subscribers are above 100,000. Alisha Marie is a good example of a macro influencer on YouTube, with a subscriber count that goes beyond 11 million. Her focus is on all things lifestyles.

The advantages of macro-influencers are that their audience is broad, and they are more experienced as far as brand partnerships are concerned. Macro-influencers are associated with higher costs for running the show. Another possible disadvantage is low engagement rates. As you might have noticed in the Alisha Marie example, macro influencers are relatively broad. They do not narrow down to a certain niche and that makes it difficult for them to engage with their audience on a personal level.

Micro-Influencers and Engagement Rate

Content creators who have between 10,000 and 100,000 subscribers are referred to as micro-influencers. Think of Riley Marie as a micro-influencer with 57,800 subscribers. Riley Marie's content is married down to books, as well as bookish challenges. Such a niche-oriented approach is usually associated with a higher audience engagement rate.

This is because the numbers of their subscribers are not too big so they can create more personal relationships with their audience. This is also an advantage in the sense that when brands look for content creators to partner with, they prefer someone who is well-connected to their audience.

In essence, micro-influencers may have lower exposure, mainly due to the lower subscriber count but their engagement and conversion rates are relatively higher. Other advantages of being a micro-influencer are the lower associated costs, the ability to focus on and reach a targeted audience, as well as authentic engagement.

How Audience Engagement Rate Is Affected by the Subscriber Counts

Now you have an idea of how audience engagement is affected by influencer statuses, whether micro or macro. Let's look further into the nitty-gritty of the relationship between subscriber counts and audience engagement rates.

Engagement rates reflect the fraction of an influencer's audience, presented as a percentage, that actively engages with the published content. What YouTube regards as engagement are the metrics such as comments and likes. For instance, if you have 500,000 subscribers, and 5,000 of these add comments or "likes" on your content, then your engagement rate becomes 10%. So, to calculate the engagement rate, use this formula:

Engagement rate = (Engagement in the form of likes and comments) ÷ (Total number of subscribers) x 100

Now, based on the calculations that are used to get the engagement rate, a micro-influencer with 50,000 subscribers needs 5,000 likes or comments for them to have a 10% engagement rate. For a macro influencer with 150,000 subscribers to get the same engagement rate, they need 50,000 comments and likes. Even though the micro-influencer has fewer subscribers, their personal connection with the audience makes it easier for them to get higher engagement rates.

This means that more of their subscribers genuinely connect and relate to the content, which is why they engage. In the case of macro-influencers, some people may just subscribe for the sake of it, maybe just to see what is happening. Some may just want to hook up with the celebrity kind of lifestyle that is associated with macro-influencers, but they are less likely to pause and comment or add a "like."

If you are wondering which engagement rate is good enough for any influencer, check the table below:

Range	Engagement Rate Category
Less than 1%	Low
1% to 3.5%	Average/Good
3.5% to 6%	High
Over 6%	Very high

Calculating the YouTube Engagement Rate

From the previous section, you probably have an idea of how to calculate the engagement rate. You should also know that there are free engagement rate calculators that you can use. However, it is also good to understand how you can calculate the engagement rate manually.

Why Is the YouTube Engagement Rate Important?

You could be having questions like, "What if I just ignore the engagement rate?" "Would the engagement rate matter much, considering that there are other metrics that I can use to assess my progress on YouTube?" or "To what extent does the engagement rate help me to improve my growth on YouTube?" We will answer all these questions in this section where we look at the reasons why you should not always keep your engagement rate in check and work toward improving it.

To Gain the Favor of the YouTube Algorithm

The YouTube algorithm is the one that ranks your content for suggestions in searches. This algorithm determines whether your content will be loved by potential viewers or not. It also takes note of whether those who have been in contact with your videos like them or not. So, although there are other metrics that are used to assess the performance of your content on YouTube, the engagement rate is the most important of all.

Therefore, when the YouTube algorithm detects a higher engagement rate on your channel, it will promote your videos so that they are seen by more members of the YouTube audience. This is because YouTube is a business—it prefers to boost the appearance of quality videos throughout the platform, so its YouTube algorithm assumes that bigger engagement rates are a sign of quality content.

To Assess the Relevance of Already Published Videos Over Time

Once you have published a video on YouTube, you should progressively evaluate its performance. You want to know if they are still growing in popularity or if they are rather declining. You can easily determine such information by checking the engagement rate patterns on your videos. You will then know where you need to take further action to enhance the way viewers relate to your content. For example, you can then decide to update the information on the videos or the thumbnails and titles.

Tips for Boosting Audience Engagement

Did you know that you can have an engagement rate of 97.4% in likes and positive comments instead of dislikes? You can achieve this if you implement the right strategies, such as the ones that we will discuss in this section.

Be Acquainted With Your Engagement Baseline

The first step that you should take in improving interaction with your viewers is knowing your current engagement rate. At least, you will have tangible numbers to work with as you create new goals that take engagement rates to the next level. To properly evaluate the engagement rate, here are some of the metrics that you will have to consider:

- **The like-to-dislike rates:** This describes the ratio of likes versus dislikes. This rate is regarded as good if the value is above 97.4%.

- **The comment-to-view rate:** This highlights the number of people who watched your videos and left comments. The percentage between 0.04% and 0.16% is considered to be good.

- **The view-to-subscriber rate:** This assesses the number of views on a video against the sum of the subscribers. Interestingly, it is good when it exceeds 33.1%.

- **The like-to-view rate:** This shows you the percentage of people who "liked" your content after watching your videos.

Now, how best can you use such metrics to determine your way forward with regard to increasing engagement with your content? Let's suppose that you have a like-to-dislike rate of, say, 98% and a view-to-subscriber rate of 5%, what would you make out of this? Actually, this is a good sign. The like-to-dislike rate shows that people are in love with what you are publishing on YouTube.

However, for some reason, they are not subscribing. Some might just be reluctant to do so, so you need to come up with practical ways to encourage them to subscribe. Still using the same scenario, let's assume that the comment-to-view rate is 0.01%, which is quite low. Again, considering that the like-to-dislike rate is high, it could be just that the viewers forgot to leave a comment, or they enjoyed the content on your playlist so much that they simply jumped from one video to the next. Interact with them and give them more solid reasons to pause and leave a comment.

Find Out More About the Audience

Could it be that there is something that you have been missing with regard to your audience on YouTube? There is no harm in using YouTube Analytics to discover more of your target audience's characteristics so that you can explore them to your advantage and increase engagement. Here are some important attributes that you should look at during your assessment:

- **The average time that they spend watching content that is similar to yours:** This helps you to determine the length of the videos that you publish. Viewers who have very busy lifestyles might prefer shorter and straight-to-the-point videos. Videos that are too long might repel their attention, so they are less likely to engage under such circumstances.

- **How they consider videos to watch:** Does your audience trust video suggestions that are provided by YouTube? Could it be that they prefer to select videos from the results on search engines? Know how the people who are most likely to view your content choose videos to watch and twitch your work accordingly.

- **The devices they use for watching videos:** Assess the type of devices that your viewers use when watching content. Those who use mobile phones can comment and like your content anywhere and at any time because the devices are portable and so can be carried around. People who use computers might have restricted times when they can watch and engage with your videos.

- **Viewers' information:** Not all content is equally relevant for all people. Therefore, you might need to consider factors such as geographical location and age of the audience. For instance, a colorful video about making cupcakes may not be appealing to everyone but should instead be targeted to a younger audience interested in learning how to bake.

Trigger or Request for the Interaction

You might be surprised to know that some of the people who are enjoying your content simply forget to engage in the way that is recognized by the YouTube algorithm. They might laugh, verbally share the information that they get from your videos, or even invite friends to watch along with them. Unfortunately, you won't be able to benefit from that type of engagement. You can cause this type of audience to like or comment on your videos by asking for interaction.

You could do this just in the same way you ask the YouTube audience to subscribe to your content. You can even add questions or comments that will urge them to comment. Please note that it is normal if it feels a bit cringy when you do it, especially for the first time. Keep on, you will get over it, while you increase the comments, likes, and shares for your videos.

Create Custom Thumbnails

Sometimes, content creators fall in love with certain things that represent their brands and forget that they are not making those for themselves but for the audience. So, you should avoid getting into such a trap because if you do, you won't realize that people do not seem to be attracted. This concept also applies to thumbnails. Changing or updating them might open doors to better opportunities for audience engagement.

Engage With Your Audience

Your audience is more likely to engage more if you begin interactions with them. Don't just wait for them to start liking, commenting, and sharing your content without you connecting to them, otherwise, their activity might become short-lived. Create and nurture a long-lasting bond between your viewers and your brand and this will help you to have a loyal audience that is engaging.

Usually, it is easier for you to interact with your audience when it is still relatively small. For instance, you could easily engage with, say, 8,500 subscribers to your channel than you would if you had 100,000 of them. We recommend that you do everything possible to continue communicating with your audience, no matter how big the community becomes.

Leave some comments, ask them for their views, and give them meaningful call-to-action. As you continue to engage with your audience, remember that the attributes that describe them may change over time. As a result, their likes and goals for watching your content might also change. Be sure to take note of such transitions and respond accordingly.

Don't Be Numb to Changing Trends

Research and connect to changing trends that are relevant to you and your community. That skill of being able to match what is currently happening is one of the sure ways to keep your audience curious about more of your content, thereby keeping them connected to your brand. However, you should be careful not to use click baits to attract the attention of viewers. Keeping up with trends is good but you need to maintain authenticity and integrity in the process.

Peep Into the Strategy Packages of Competitors

Sometimes, you can derive the best practices that attract more engagement from others. This is especially true when you think you have exhausted your ideas. Go to other channels that are in the same niche as you and learn as much as you can. Check the videos that are associated with more audience engagement and look at their format.

Evaluate their visuals, sounds, text, and coordination. How do they respond to the comments of viewers? Do they even respond to negative comments at all? If yes, how do they handle rude, diminishing, and miscalculated comments? Please remember that the reason why you are browsing through the channels of your competitors is not for you to imitate their content. You are there to get insights on how you can be in a better position to enhance audience engagement.

Use Calls-To-Action

You might need to check how you end your videos. Do you leave the audience with a task that boosts engagement? If not, this is something that you can improve on, and the possible results may be quite amazing. Calls to action can be added as you begin or end your video. For example, you could say, "If you found this video interesting, please don't forget to give it a thumbs-up before you leave."

You could even pose a question and then say, "Please, leave your opinion in the comments section." Always try by all means to ensure that your calls-to-action are well-weaved into the rest of the video. Don't make it look like it's just popping from nowhere. That kind of detachment can shun the viewers off and they won't engage.

Position Yourself Well for the YouTube SEO

Have you ever heard of the saying, "If you can't beat them, join them"? This relates well to the idea of incorporating relevant keywords that make your videos appear at the top of the list of results that pop up when viewers insert search words in YouTube's search engines. If you have neglected this area before, it's time to join the winning team by using the right keywords.

Of course, this comes with some research so that you know the words and phrases that YouTube will probably use when they search for the type of content that you publish. When you use appropriate keywords, the chances that your content will appear in suggested videos also increase. As the traffic to your videos increases, you might also stand a better chance to have more likes, comments, and subscriptions.

Pay More Attention to Your Video Editing Process

You should always keep in mind the fact that there are many videos at your audience's disposal. They could watch those, instead of yours, so once you manage to get them to watch your content, get that opportunity to use it. Any unnecessary disappointment will drive them to other channels with similar content.

You need to work on retaining the viewers to your channel for the longest possible time, which increases the probability of increased engagement. One of the effective strategies that you can employ in getting this done is properly editing your videos. Cut off any form of fluff that might frustrate your viewers.

Come Up With a More Frequent and Consistent Publishing Schedule

At one point or the other, you will have new visitors coming to your channel. You don't want them to enjoy your content and then realize that you only publish a video after every four and a half months. This will simply put them off and that would be one opportunity for possible audience engagement to be lost. So, there are two factors that matter here, which are, the frequency at which you publish your videos and the consistency with which you do so. Ideally, don't take too long before adding another piece of your content.

Weekly schedules are good. Once you decide to publish on a weekly basis, for example, please do so consistently. You could simply pick a day during which you will add new videos and stick with that. Your viewers should rest assured that a new release is coming every Thursday night, for example. This is a great way to foster engagement.

Collaborate With Fellow YouTubers

Collaborating with other YouTubers gives you the leverage to extend your reach to more people. However, you need to be careful of who you collaborate with if the venture is going to be fruitful. If your niche is on fashion and design, joining hands with another YouTuber whose focus is on gardening is unlikely to yield the desired results.

Collaborate with someone whose niche overlaps well with yours such that there is something common in the interests of the audiences involved. For example, people who are interested in cooking, in general, might also find baking tutorials interesting. In this case, a collaboration could cause an increased engagement through a "cross-pollination" kind of process.

Consider Using Hashtags

Did you know that using hashtags in videos aids in increased visibility on the YouTube platform? All you have to do is to incorporate hashtags in the titles and descriptions of your videos. These hashtags tell the targeted audience more about what your video is all about before they click on it to watch. This strategy helps you to attack only the people who are interested in your content. The probability that such people will comment, like, share, or subscribe to your content is relatively high. We recommend that you use broader hashtags so that a broader range of viewers can visit your channel and watch your videos.

Consider YouTube Shorts

For some reason, short videos are the current trend, from TikTok to YouTube. Considering that YouTube is investing much in YouTube Shorts, hooking up with the trend could see you earning more viewers and possibly greater audience engagement.

Go for Live Streaming

Go live and engage more with the people who matter most to your YouTube business. Live streaming gives you more time to hang out with your audience so that you engage in deeper interactions at a more personal level. This way, your audience will not only connect with your brand and content, but they will bond with you as a person. Audience engagement can increase this way.

It's another moment to go practical! Presented in this section is a checklist that assists you to track your progress in implementing the various strategies that can contribute to increasing audience engagement. Simply tick on each of the tips that you would have implemented and write a comment on what exactly you did and the results that you noted if any. For strategies that you will not implement at all, use the comment section to explain your reasons.

This chapter has shown that the importance of audience engagement cannot be overemphasized. It's comparable to one of the components of the blood that keeps humans alive. Without audience engagement, your business cannot grow, and monetizing it becomes even more difficult. Therefore, you need to tune in to the mindset of growing the engagement rate for your video. Talking of "mindsets," the next chapter touches on the correct mindset that will enhance success in your venture as a YouTube content creator.

Checklist

	Collaborate with other YouTubers.
	Produce YouTube shorts.
	Improve the editing process if possible.
	Use hashtags.
	Lowkey borrow ideas from other channels.
	Create custom thumbnails.
	Do constant research about your audience.
	Host live streams.

Keep up engagement with your viewers.
Use calls-to-action.
Establish a sustainable publishing schedule and adjust as needed.

Chapter 6:

The Mindset You Need to Achieve Success on YouTube

Positive traits like being achievement-focused and orderly are not evenly distributed among humans. There are some individuals who seem to be able to do this effortlessly. The difference between these people and the rest is that they have the success mindset that helps them to thrive on challenges and not allow failure to describe them.

People with a positive mindset see failure as a springboard for growth and make use of every opportunity to develop their abilities. Growth is a natural trait in humans, and with such a mindset, you can enjoy increased viewership and eventually achieve success.

This chapter focuses mainly on helping you to cultivate a mindset that will get you to achieve success on YouTube. Success is more easily achieved with practice and time. More often than not, people have started YouTube channels that they have eventually abandoned because they lack the proper mindset to achieve success.

Having a success mindset helps you with content planning and with extending your viewership until your page becomes successful. This chapter will help you with cultivating such a vital mindset.

The Growth Mindset for Achieving Success on YouTube

The growth mindset is key to achieving success on YouTube. In contrast to a fixed mindset, the growth mindset is a mindset that believes that an individual's abilities can be developed over time. The growth mindset is that mindset that believes that it is possible to achieve something better. That mindset is open to effort and believes that by working hard, better results can come.

Why Is It Important to Have a Growth Mindset for Success?

The kind of mindset that a person has affects the lifestyle of that individual. When you have a growth mindset, you have the passion to learn, and you do not hunger for the approval of others. With a growth mindset, you believe that there is a chance for improvement in everything, including intelligence, creativity, friendships and associations, and performance. All this is made possible by patience and practice. When they exercise a growth mindset, individuals are happier and more content.

A growth mindset is important because it helps you to:

- **Accept failure and embrace imperfection:** A growth mindset improves your ability to respond to challenges. When you take on challenges, you allow yourself to struggle and even fail, while maintaining a positive stance. The need for you to think critically in turn incites growth in your skills and abilities. As a content creator and YouTube account holder, you will need to try out new things and experience flops and failures, while viewing each as a learning curve. After failure, a growth mindset helps you to develop new strategies and make multiple attempts until you achieve success. Instead of labeling imperfection as undesirable, and viewing it as a dead end, you learn to celebrate the challenges you faced and the resultant growth.

- **Trust the process:** The growth mindset has a full understanding that the pathway to success is long and challenging. The achievement of success on YouTube is process oriented. When you place value on the process more than on the result, you are more patient and will be able to learn and make necessary changes along the way. Having a fixed mindset sees you as being result-oriented and often leads to taking shortcuts. If ever success is achieved in that manner, it is short-lived. A growth mindset, in contrast, is ready to go all the way, step by step, and believes that success will be met along the way.

- **Remain relevant in a fast-paced world:** Considering how fast-paced the world has become, having a growth mindset has never been more important. Every single day, there are new things to learn and new challenges to tackle. New trends are coming into play on a daily basis, and you have to continuously research what type of content is more captivating at any given time. Ways of life and norms are changing, and individuals have to adjust accordingly in order to stay relevant. This is why it is very important to steer clear of a fixed mindset and be flexible enough to adjust to the changes that are happening in technological, social, and economic changes that are happening every day.

Misconceptions About the Growth Mindset

In many major companies and organizations, "growth mindset" has become a key phrase, and it has since been incorporated into some mission statements. However, many people have a limited understanding of the growth mindset and often present some misconceptions about it. This section details some of the misconceptions that people have about the growth mindset and seeks to set the record straight.

A Growth Mindset Is All About Rewarding Effort

This is especially true for employees in different organizations. If a growth mindset is all about rewarding effort, this is quite inaccurate because outcomes matter. Effort can either be productive or unproductive and if it is unproductive, it is not a good thing. If the effort is rewarded, it has to be coupled with learning and progress. The processes that yield progress have to be emphasized within an organization, and these include trying out new strategies, getting help from others, and learning from mistakes. When these are mastered well, we can then say a growth mindset has been implemented within the organization.

I Already Have a Growth Mindset

Being flexible or open-minded is altogether different from having a growth mindset. Having a positive outlook also does not qualify as having a growth mindset. People who have these qualities tend to think that they have a growth mindset, although it is often termed a false growth mindset. The truth is that everyone presents a mixture of growth and fixed mindsets, and this mixture evolves with time. In a good case, the growth mindset eventually overpowers the fixed mindset. Such an individual has a better chance of achieving success.

When You Have a Growth Mindset, Good Things Will Happen

The importance of mission statements owes to the fact that you cannot argue with vital values like empowerment, growth, and innovation. These values, however, have to be real and attainable, so you have to implement policies to make them achievable. Organizations that support a growth mindset are open to risk-taking, with the full knowledge that some risks will not work out.

They support teamwork in the place of competition and focus on the lessons learned, even if the attempt does not lead to the achievement of goals. The growth of every single member brings joy to the organization. The general idea is that with a growth mindset, you are open to good or bad things happening out of your attempts, and both bring you joy because you are able to draw out lessons from each venture.

Even if we make efforts to clear these misconceptions, it is still not easy to achieve a growth mindset. One of the major reasons for this is that every individual has a fixed mindset trigger. When we come across challenges or do poorly in comparison to others, we tend to become defensive and insecure, and this does not encourage growth. In most cases, it is all about competition.

The Neuroscience of a Growth Mindset

More than 30 years ago, a study was carried out by Carol Dweck and her colleagues. The study was an attempt to determine the attitudes of students about failure. The observation was that there were some students who rebounded after failure and others that seemed so devastated by the smallest of setbacks.

Having carried this study through, the terms fixed mindset and growth mindset were then coined. Advances in neuroscience that have been taking place have proven that the brain is malleable more than we ever imagined.

Research has been carried out on the plasticity of the brain. The study has shown that the connectivity between neurons changes with experience. The neural networks grow new connections with practice, or the existing networks are strengthened, and insulation is built that speeds up the transmission of impulses. The results from neuroscientific studies show that humans are able to increase their neural growth depending on the actions they take. These actions include the use of good strategies, practicing, asking questions, good sleeping habits, as well as good nutrition.

With more of these studies carried out, the link between mindsets and achievement was eventually established. It turns out that people who believe that their brains can grow to behave differently in comparison to those that do not. The question of whether or not mindsets can be changed led to further research and the establishment that it is indeed possible to change the mindset from fixed to growth. When this happens, the result is often increased achievement and motivation.

People with a growth mindset are mostly fixed on development, even if it may take time. These people completely detest the fixed mindset, which is less focused on success. People with fixed mindsets are fixated on non-positive thoughts like, "I am good for nothing," or "I always fail." These people are convinced that nothing can be done about their current state and that it is too late for them to try anything. Even if it is not too late, they believe that trying is a waste of effort because they think they will still fail anyway.

Whenever people with a fixed mindset are faced with a task, they tend to think that it is very hard to accomplish, and they often struggle through it. When they look at other people, they are made to feel inferior because the success of the people around them is seemingly easy. People with a growth mindset, on the other hand, are more eager to grab opportunities and do so with the belief that they are perfect for the job.

When they encounter failure, people with a growth mindset are not derailed, they try again until they achieve their goals. Failure, to them, is not a signal to stop, but rather a signal to put more effort next time around. Persistence is a key feature of the growth mindset.

Developing a Growth Mindset

Developing a growth mindset is not an easy task, although it is quite worth the effort. It is not only a better way to improve the learning process but also a better way to improve life in general. In order to develop a growth mindset, there is a need to cultivate self-acceptance within yourself. You should be confident enough to believe that you are capable of accomplishing the task.

You should condition your mind to accept failure, and learn from it so that you avoid it the next time. Most people view failure as inability. You need to redefine what failure means to you. When attempting something new, you must have conviction within yourself, and avoid seeking the approval of others. Your self-confidence is enough on its own.

The growth mindset is a term that is mostly used in the world of education, especially when looking for ways to improve academic performance. However, it has become relevant to be applied in the circular world, as the mindset is important even in the business world. Often, we find ourselves experiencing fixed mindsets, although they can be adjusted. For instance, someone may describe themselves as not being a "math person" so as to avoid it. When you do that, you avoid momentary struggle and failure with this excuse and delay development.

A person with a growth mindset is willing to try difficult things, and in doing so they learn and develop their skill set to perfection. Even if they struggle, a person with a growth mindset will still find joy in trying again because they know they have the potential to do better and are excited at the chance to get it right. As such, the probability of maximizing their potential is quite high because of their ability to learn from mistakes, take on challenges head-on, and accept criticism.

Growth Mindset Activities for Adults

As an adult, and a person who is hungry for success, not only should you focus on the creation of a healthy environment, but you should also indulge in growth mindset activities. These activities help you to develop yourself further while enjoying the process at the same time. The following section will explore some of the growth mindset activities that you can engage in.

Self-Exploration

With a fixed mindset, the chances that in the next 10 years, you will be stuck in the same position that you are in now are quite high. The current mindset has a bearing on how we shape our future. Self-exploration is a process whereby you go deep into yourself and start working on your mindset. To help you do that, you can start by watching a two-minute video called "Lost Generation."

The general idea is to learn how the future is set based on the attitude you adopt today. Self-exploration and determining what happens in our lives and to the future when we change our mindsets can be done in a group, or if that is not possible, you can still do it by yourself.

Identify Everyday Mindset Examples

Both fixed mindsets and growth mindsets are experienced every single day. You are more likely to develop a growth mindset when you actively engage yourself in identifying which type of mindset and behavior you present when facing daily tasks. One way to go about this is to write down examples of how you can apply each mindset to everyday life.

You can do so by writing down your opinion on subjects like failure, challenges, and adversity. For this activity to be worthwhile, you need to understand both mindsets. If possible, you can do this activity in a group, and discuss your thoughts with each other.

Take Action

The easiest growth mindset activity you can do is to simply take action. The toughest part of taking action is starting something new or trying to build a habit. With a fixed mindset, you will not be that eager to step out of your comfort zone, but if you want to develop a growth mindset, you will need a change of attitude and gear yourself to start doing more. One way to do this is to try and tackle tough tasks that you have otherwise always avoided and avoid focusing on the stuff that you are already passionate about. Exploring new passions helps you to try out things that you otherwise would never have thought of.

Actively Look for Opportunities to Learn

Within your industry, or outside of it, you can start looking for opportunities that you previously thought you didn't fit into. Often, the things that you are hesitant to try often give you the opportunity to learn. This is because it teaches you a very important trait of learning to be comfortable with being uncomfortable. You learn the importance of your attitude in determining your success. Learning in a new area makes you knowledgeable in that field, and continuous learning brings you a step closer to being proficient, even if you might not be a professional. That is the confidence you need to make it to success on YouTube.

Develop Grit

Grit is the effort that you put into the work that you do, overcoming obstacles and persisting. It is the definition of your persistence in the attempt to meet the goals that you set for yourself. Developing your grit may have to do with you finding a specific area that you want to focus on and continue finding ways to do better at it. It is also very wise to surround yourself with people that have grit if you want to develop it too. Spending most of your time around people that show up every day and stick to their goals will have you become like them over time.

Playful Learning

To start with, you can try to figure out things that intrigue you. You can try things like juggling or Sudoku. Some activities take a considerable time to learn, and you need to be patient to learn them. In doing so, you are building patience and cultivating a growth mindset. Anything that challenges you in a satisfactory manner is good for you to try. One good thing to do is to try and refresh your routines. For example, if you are into painting or cooking, try a new painting or cook a new dish that you have never worked on before. If you are into running, try a new route. Try shaking up your day a little with a new activity.

30-Day Challenge

The development of the growth mindset can be fun if you decide to make the process so. You can break down the activities that you choose for the development of the mindset into 30-day challenges. This is one great way to establish habits that help you to develop a growth mindset.

Draw Inspiration From Others

There are so many examples of people who have successfully developed growth mindsets and have achieved success in different areas. It is good for you to draw inspiration from them and try to follow in their footsteps. It is an honorable habit to embrace and learn about the success of others. It does not necessarily have to be big names. There are people within your network who can inspire you so make sure you identify them and spend more time with them.

Be Curious

Curiosity and growth go hand in hand, and you should make them part of your daily routine. You should be able to ask big and open questions. This is a strong foundation for the growth mindset. Asking questions is good for cultivating your curiosity, at the same time encouraging those people around you to share their ideas and thoughts with you. This gives you a great opportunity to learn.

Seek Feedback

Feedback is the heart of cultivating a growth mindset. Feedback is constructive and integral to your development. You need to come up with ways of getting feedback from the people that you spend time with. Getting feedback can be part of your daily routine and be sure to make use of the feedback to learn and grow. In seeking feedback, make sure you are a great listener and be ready to embrace both positive and negative feedback.

Embracing and Improving Your Growth Mindset to Achieve Success

A growth mindset, as has been made clear in this book, does not come magically, but is rather something that you have to work for. Through effort and experience, we can improve our abilities and learn new things. You cannot master anything unless you apply energy to it. Mental and physical repetition of a routine is how growth is eventually achieved.

When you are faced with a challenge, you can choose to reframe and have a positive mindset. Believe that if you practice multiple times, it is possible to improve your skills at anything. Of course, building a growth mindset takes hard work, but hard work is always rewarding.

You should develop a positive mindset, one that believes it is possible. Instead of asking yourself a question like "Did I do well?" you can ask, "What can I do to improve next time?" This means that you focus on what you can do to improve, not on how you are perceived. It is wise to invest your time and effort in developing a mindset that propels you toward success.

There are several challenges that you will experience in building wealth through YouTube, and you have to embrace a growth mindset to go through them. You have to believe that you are a powerful force, and you can do hard things. When you meet obstacles in your way, tell yourself that you will come out of it a better person, and it is going to be easier the next time.

Having an attitude that embraces growth is very crucial for the achievement of success on YouTube. In this section are tips that help you to embrace the growth mindset.

Practice Gratitude

The impact of being grateful on your overall outlook is often underrated. When you learn to acknowledge what you are thankful for helps to shift your mindset to a positive one. Focusing on the good things that are happening to you helps you to worry less about the things that you do not have or did not go your way.

See Problems as Challenges

Facing adversity is normal in life and in business. The mindset with which you tackle adversity is what is important. It determines whether you will grow as a result of the challenge or will stall out. Your perspective changes completely when you begin to see roadblocks as challenges, instead of as problems. If you see them as problems that have to be fixed, you will probably cower away, but if you see them as challenges to be accomplished, you gear yourself.

Choose to Be Successful and Embrace the Journey

Being successful is a decision that you have to make, and it helps you to embrace the road ahead. You should be willing to try out new avenues and be open to making mistakes along the way. When you view business development as a journey, you are more expectant of new opportunities and experiences. Occasionally, you will fail or falter, but you will be better able to rebound when you embrace the growth mindset.

Celebrate Your Successes

Successful YouTube entrepreneurs celebrate their successes. When you encounter a new prospect, celebrate it. Those baby steps are very important. When you focus too much on the successes of others, you lose focus on your goal. When you make small wins, revel in your victory and allow yourself to feel the joy over your success. That growth mindset and being grateful fuels your next move and keeps you going.

Change How You Speak

The way you speak says volumes about the type of mindset that you have. Essentially, you should learn to avoid the language that emphasizes limitations and inability. You need to be more positive in your language. For example, you can incorporate the word "yet" in statements that would otherwise reflect impossibility.

This means that instead of saying, "People are not subscribing to my channel," rather say, "People are not yet subscribing to my channel." Instead of "I don't have the equipment that makes quality videos," why not say, "I don't have the equipment that produces the quality of videos that I want yet." Please note that changing to this kind of language is not a "one-day" event. It is a process that might take some time, but with constant practice, you will certainly get there.

Focus More on the Process, Than the Results

As a YouTuber, focus more on the process of coming up with ideas for your content, producing your videos, uploading them, and putting together strategies that enhance visibility and audience engagement. Let your passion take its toll as you enjoy the process. Be authentic and do everything to deliver your best.

While the results are also important, they should not be your focal point. Sometimes, concentrating on results may bring frustration if you don't get the outcomes that you were expecting. If you focus on the process, the better results always come as a surprise and that could motivate you to do better next time.

Don't Cover Up Your Weaknesses

No matter the level that you are in growing a growth mindset, there is no point in hiding your weaknesses. Rather identify and acknowledge them so that you can find a way to deal with them. If you don't address your weaknesses, they will get in your way of developing a growth mindset. If you are impatient, you can only subdue that attribute for some time. However, there will come times when you simply can't keep retaking a video to perfect it—that would be impatience taking over. Facing your weaknesses head-on is another way of nurturing a growth mindset.

Understand That Learning Goals Are Better Than Performance Goals

The types of goals that you set for yourself reflect the kind of mindset that you have. In fact, information from research highlighted that people with growth mindsets embrace goals that are related to learning, like improving certain skills. On the contrary, a fixed mindset focuses more on performance goals like hitting performance key indicators (KPIs).

Are you wondering why that matters? When you concentrate on performance goals, you limit your mind to short-term success and at the end of it all, you will simply feel like you have either passed or failed. After that, what then? On the other hand, learning goals yield results that have long-term positive effects.

Now, let's apply this concept to your YouTube business. When you create and publish your content, you might set a performance goal of getting 1,000 subscriptions within a month. On the other hand, you could set up a learning goal of increasing the quality of your content and engaging more with your audience. The first goal is good but the motivation that is associated with it is relatively short-term.

Once you get 1,000 subscribers, you feel that you have achieved what you want and are done. If you fail to, you might get discouraged and probably give up. Increasing the quality of your content and engaging your audience can be done for a lifetime, meaning that they are long-term goals. You can still get 1,000 subscribers and even more if you work toward these learning-oriented goals.

Exercises That Enhance a Growth Mindset

As you might have realized, developing and nurturing a growth mindset is a continuous process. As time progresses, your mindset becomes more growth-oriented and flexible than fixed. There are some mental exercises and games that can help you in your endeavor to make your mindset more growth-oriented and we will explore some of them in this section.

The "Three Positive Things" Challenge

This is an exercise that you should do on a daily basis. All you have to do is notice three things related to your work on YouTube that have had a positive impact on yourself, your team, or your audience. It doesn't matter how small things appear to be. Could it be that you were able to meet up at the agreed time for a video shoot? Or maybe it's another publishing Wednesday and you have just unleashed another killer video for your beloved audience. Such consistency is worth noticing. Practicing having an eye for positivity is a great way for retraining your brain to embrace the growth opportunities that come with change.

Meditate More Often

Just in the same way that you work out to strengthen other muscles of your body, you should also meditate to increase your brain's resilience. Remember, your brain is also a muscle, though it is often ignored as far as exercising is concerned. There are various tools that can assist you to get started with meditation and Headspace is one of them. Here, we will take you through a simple meditation procedure that you can consider practicing more often. Here are the steps:

1. Find a quiet place to reduce the chances of getting disturbed.

2. Sit down in a manner that is comfortable to you—it could be on a chair or bench, or the floor.

3. Gently close your eyes just so you can concentrate on the meditation procedure. Make sure your arms are resting comfortably, with your spine and neck straight, not bent.

4. Now, slowly breathe in to count to five. While holding your breath, say, "Every mistake is my opportunity to learn and get better."

5. Slowly breathe out and then say, "My mistakes are not a sign of failure."

Each time you breathe in, say something positive about yourself and your YouTube business. After breathing out, mention an aspect of the fixed mindset that you don't want. Continue as much as you can. When you are done, simply open your eyes and reconnect to the environment. Set aside time to meditate regularly. This activity does not need much time, even 5 or 10 minutes per day will do.

If you haven't tried it yet, even Bill Gates was once in that same state as you. Here is what he had to say:

> I thought of meditation as a woo-woo thing tied somehow to reincarnation, and I didn't buy into it. I now see that meditation is simply exercise for the mind, similar to the way we exercise our muscles when we play sports. (para. 2)

As of now, Gates meditates two to three times every week.

The "Escaping the Echo Chambers" Game

This game is based on the idea by Adam Grant in his book called *Think Again*. In this book, Grant suggested that an "echo chamber" is where everyone around agrees with your thoughts, views, statements, and probably everything else. Therefore, you should get into a discussion where you take one side of the story, and your opponent takes another.

Challenge your opponent and try to make them see your side of the story and they will obviously be doing all they can to make you hear them, instead. As this happens, don't just concentrate on beating them in the argument, also try to learn from their viewpoint. Here are the major questions that you should ask yourself after the discussion:

- Is there anything new that you learned from the discussion? What could that be?

- Based on the discussion, do you think you can alter the way you used to see things?

The "Mindset Assessment" Game

In this game, the idea is for you to see if your mindset is more of a fixed or growth one. You should do it as a group. Create cards that have various scenarios and place them in a bowl. One of you should then pick one of the cards and read what is written on it. Every other member of the group present should then say their thoughts on how they would possibly tackle the situation. Let everyone try to be as honest as possible. You will then help each other to evaluate, from the given responses, whether one has a growth or fixed mindset. Here are some examples of the scenarios that you can write on the cards:

- Your spouse receives an invitation to a party from their ex-boyfriend or ex-girlfriend.

- In your comments section on YouTube, a member of the audience writes, "This is not a place for cowboys. If you don't know how to create good videos, disappear from space."

- You've been retaking a 10-minute video for more than 2 hours now. You are now at a point where you are making the best shot of them all and then eight minutes into the shooting, the microphone stops working.

Recite Growth Mindset Affirmations

Positive affirmations can transform your way of thinking as time goes on. Therefore, you can use them to change your mindset. Here are some growth mindset affirmations that you can consider reciting on a daily basis:

- I can do anything, regardless of the level of difficulty.

- If there's something that I don't do well, it's only because I am yet to find how it's properly done.

- I am always ready to do my best and today, I will do that again.

- I always want to learn new things because I know that I get better in the process.

- I don't run away from challenges because they are opportunities for improvement.

Reading Anything

Get into the habit of reading, be it books, poems, news, novels, you name it. The more you read, the wider your mind becomes, and this aids flexibility. Reading allows you to learn more so it helps you to nurture a growth mindset.

Go for Physical Exercise

Did you know that exercise can also have a positive impact on your mind? It increases your self-esteem and sense of control, both of which are essential components of a growth mindset. This happens in various ways. For example, when you exercise, your brain releases more hormones like serotonin which helps the brain and nerve cells to function well.

Endorphins, which are hormones that are associated with improving your mood, while reducing stress and pain are also produced in larger amounts when you exercise. Moreover, exercise simply increases the energy levels in your body, which is good because then you can better tackle the activities that are related to your goals.

Another reason why exercising is great for your brain's health is that it increases the connections between nerve cells in the brain. Your brain's functionality is improved when its nerve cells create more associations. This way, your brain will function in a more balanced way, thereby making it easier to deal with emotional aspects such as depression, fear, and anxiety.

Therefore, be sure to exercise as many times as you can. The types of workouts that you engage in do not really matter at this point—just exercises. Jogging, walking on the pavement, stretching, rope skipping, and cycling are just a few of the exercises that you can do.

A growth mindset is something that you cannot do without in any venture, even in your business as a content creator on YouTube. This is why implementing the strategies that we outlined in this chapter is crucial. In this section, you will find two checklists. The first will highlight various strategies that you can use to grow, nurture, and maintain a growth mindset. All you have to do is tick the applicable response to show whether you have implemented the suggestion or not.

You can also comment on your progress and possible results in the "comments" section. The second checklist will highlight the exercises that you can try in a bid to assist your brain to adopt a growth mindset more. If you have started doing the activities that are highlighted in the list, also fill in the frequency at which you do them and comment on any progress that you are noticing.

The growth mindset is vital throughout the journey, from coming up with ideas for creating your content to getting the videos published. You will also need a growth mindset when it comes to monetizing your channel. In the next chapter, we will zero in on how you can earn from your hard work as a YouTuber.

Checklist

	Engage in playful learning.
	Develop and adopt positive speaking.
	Go for learning goals rather than performance goals.
	Identify your weaknesses and work at them.
	Celebrate your successes, no matter how small!
	Seek feedback.
	Look for learning opportunities.

Do 'growth mindset' games and exercises.

Chapter 7:

Monetizing Your YouTube Channel

There are different ways in which one can make an income as a content creator on YouTube. To start making money through content creation, YouTube requires a certain number of subscribers and watch time on your channel. In this chapter, we'll focus more on the different ways through which you can monetize your account, as well as the protocols that you should follow to avoid any penalties.

YouTube Guidelines and Requirements for Monetizing Your Channel

The YPP is mostly used by YouTubers. Almost every YouTuber's goal is to reach a partner status because it permits them to add advertisements to every video they post, thereby generating income. However, not everyone qualifies to reach the partner status because YouTube is very selective about who it decides to bring into the program.

When you've decided on monetizing your channel, keep in mind that it is important to follow the YouTube monetization policies such as Google AdSense program policies, terms of service, copyright, and YouTube's community guidelines. These policies apply to every content creator who wants to take part in the YPP or those who receive benefits from the YouTube Shorts Fund.

What Can Be Monetized?

This policy assures that monetized content presents unique videos for viewers to watch. Viewers should be able to identify the difference in quality between your content, in comparison to other creators. The good quality of your videos is the first step that determines that your channel can be monetized. YouTube is aware of creators that create the same content as others, and this is a form of plagiarism. Creating unique videos will let your channel stand out amongst others. There is no harm in borrowing ideas from other content creators, but your content still has to be original. There should be something new or different. For instance:

- The introduction and ending of the videos may be similar, but the content within the video should be different.

- A more in-depth discussion about the same topic in each of your videos.

- Using short clips to explain the same concepts further.

YouTube policies are used to determine if a channel qualifies for monetization, so it is important to carefully read through it. Channels that are monetized are regularly checked by commentators to see if they are following these policies.

What Commentators Look for When in Channel Reviews

Commentators check for content that violates YouTube's policies. Commentators may pay attention to your channel's:

- most viewed videos

- recent videos

- main theme

- watch time

- video metadata

It is important to know that if necessary, commentators can go through other areas of your channel to ensure that all policies are being followed.

Community Guidelines

Maintaining these guidelines helps keep a safe community for creators, advertisers, and viewers. Videos that violate the guidelines will not be monetized and in worst-case scenarios, they are removed from YouTube. If your channel has been monetized, it is important to apply the guidelines to your entire channel and not just one video.

The AdSense Policy Program

YouTube partners are given access by AdSense to get rewarded for monetizing their content. AdSense content policies are broad and include guidelines from the webmaster and search console policies. Let's go through some of the most applicable policies for YouTube content creators.

Repetition of the Same Materials

This involves adding more or less the same videos on your channel, thereby making it difficult for viewers to distinguish between them. The policy is connected to the AdSense program's Search Console section. The rule needs to be followed across the board in your channel. YouTube will stop monetizing your channel if there are multiple videos on your channel that break the rules.

Content That Cannot Be Monetized

You cannot monetize any of the following:

- content that is not created by you, also known as "unowned" content.

- music that is edited to sound unique but is not owned by you.

- content that has no value or meaning.

- slideshows that have images and text with no clear meaning.

Quality Principles for Kids and Families

This policy is there to assure not only creators but also families and kids by providing a safe and educational experience when they open YouTube. YouTube's quality principles will be applied to channels under "made for kids" and to process the channels' monetization. Your channel may lose a YouTube partner if it does not reach the "made for kids" standard when it comes to creating content. If YouTube detects that your channel has violated such quality guidelines, you're most likely to see fewer ads or none at all.

Application of Quality Principles for Monetization Eligibility

Content that promotes negative behavior and dangerous activities may have a bad impact on a specific video. Any sign of negativity promoted by your channel will be considered when processing your channel for monetization. YouTube goes against low-quality principles for children's and family content. Here are some of the aspects that they look at:

- **Promoting bad behavior and a lack of respect:** Content that promotes dangerous activities, picking on others, and lying are less likely to be monetized. This includes dangerous pranks and unhealthy lifestyles.

- **Heavily commercial or promotional:** Content that is solely focused on brand promotion and buying of products, dolls, and nourishment.

- **Deceptively educational:** Content that misleads you into thinking it contains educational value while it is the exact opposite of what it portrays on the thumbnail. For instance, a thumbnail might be titled "Learn math" or "How to read," but when subscribers view the video, they find something that is completely different, like someone's biography.

- **Hindering comprehension:** Content that lacks connecting dots, thereby making it difficult for viewers to understand it.

- **Sensational or misleading content:** Content that is invalid and based on opinion may confuse kids. Children might be misled by "keyword stuffing" or by constantly using keywords that kids mostly like.

Creator Responsibility

Reaching your goal and being part of the YPP also depend on whether advertisers would like to work with you. Maintaining a good relationship with advertisers establishes trust that will have a positive impact on your earnings. Inhumane behavior that might have a bad impact on the community is unacceptable. According to this policy, you should respect the people watching your content, as well as other creators, including advertisers. If you fail to follow the policy, your monetization rights might be temporarily turned off or your account could be deleted.

Joining the YPP

You should first submit an application for the YPP. It might take one day for YouTube to process your registration before communicating a decision. However, processing your registration might take more than a month as YouTube reviews your application. The following criteria must be met for you to be eligible for the YPP:

- Your YouTube channel should have at least 1,000 subscribers.

- You should have a total of 4,000 watch hours within the space of a year.

- You should reside in the same county as the YPP.

- An AdSense account should be connected to your channel.

- There shouldn't be any active Community Guidelines strikes on your channel.

- You must abide by the monetization policies.

- Your account should use the two-step verification on the Google account connected to your channel so that it is more secure.

Here's a list of countries and regions you can apply to for the YPP:

American Samoa	Guam	Pakistan
Algeria	Hong Kong	Papua New Guinea
Aruba	Honduras	Philippines
Argentina	Hungary	Peru
Australia	Iceland	Portugal
Azerbaijan	Indonesia	Poland
Austria	India	Qatar
Bahrain	Israel	Puerto Rico
Bermuda	Iraq	Reunion
Bangladesh	Italy	Ireland
Belgium	Jamaica	Romania
Belarus	Jordan	Singapore
Bolivia	Japan	Slovakia
Bosnia and Herzegovina	Kenya	Saudi Arabia
Bulgaria	Kazakhstan	South Africa

Brazil	Laos	Slovenia
Canada	Kuwait	Spain
Cambodia	Latvia	South Korea
Chile	Lebanon	Sweden
Cayman Islands	Liechtenstein	Sri Lanka
Costa Rica	Libya	Taiwan
Colombia	Luxembourg	Switzerland
Cyprus	Lithuania	Thailand
Croatia	Malaysia	Tanzania
Czech Republic	Macedonia	Turkey
Denmark	Martinique	Tunisia
Dominican Republic	Malta	Uganda
Ecuador	Mexico	Turks and Caicos Islands
El Salvador	Mayotte	Ukraine
Egypt	Morocco	United Arab Emirates
Finland	Montenegro	United States
Estonia	Netherlands	United Kingdom
French Guiana	Nepal	Virgin Islands
France	Nicaragua	Uruguay
Georgia	New Zealand	Venezuela
French Polynesia	Norway	Yemen

Ghana	Nigeria	Vietnam
Germany	Oman	Zimbabwe
Guatemala	Northern Mariana Islands	
Greece	Panama	

The Application Checklist

Everyone who qualifies for the entry-level can sign up for the YPP. However, your channel needs to meet some of the guidelines to be taken into account. This checklist will help you through the application process:

- First, turn on two-step verification for your Google account. This will keep your account safe by using both your password and another way of confirming your authenticity.

- Ensure that your account doesn't go against YouTube policies and guidelines and that there aren't any active Community Guidelines strikes on your channel. After your application, YouTube will review your channel to ensure that you meet YouTube guidelines and policies. If your channel is successful, you'll be accepted into the program. YouTube will continue to monitor channels that have already been accepted to make sure that they continue to abide by its guidelines and policies.

- A sum of 1,000 subscribers and 4,000 watch hours from your viewers should be present on your channel. You need to have posted a couple of videos on your channel for YouTube to assess the content on your channel. When you've reached this stage, it means you have the right amount of content on your channel. This stage will help YouTube identify and make a clear decision on whether your content best suits the requirements of the community guidelines and policies. Once you've reached this stage, you can sign up for the YPP.

- YouTube will notify you once you've accomplished the requirements to sign up for the YPP. Follow the directions to sign up once your channel qualifies for the final stage.

How to Proceed If Your Application Is Rejected

YouTube will inform you of the rules your channel violated if your application is rejected. If that's the case, there is no need to worry. YouTube will allow you to re-register after a month. While waiting for your reapplication, make efforts to improve your channel, especially with regard to areas that would have been highlighted in the rejection notification.

Enabling Monetization on YouTube

Once you become part of the YPP, enable monetization for all your videos. You can do this before posting your new content, but to avoid any technical issues, it is best that you do this after adding your videos. After a few hours, YouTube will have reviewed your content. You'll be informed if YouTube finds something in your content that goes against the Community Guidelines and policies, be it copyright claims, adult materials, and/or cursing.

Ways to Monetize Your Channel

As a YouTube content creator, keep in mind that you can benefit from a couple of things from YouTube AdSense, but do not completely depend on it when it comes to creating income. You'll not make the same amount each year because of the inconsistent advertising rates, so you might make less money at some point. That's why companies pay for every 1,000 impressions that an ad receives, also known as the cost per mile (CPM). The amount you'll be paid will differ from other content creators because of the different niches and audiences each channel presents.

If you want to make a balanced income on YouTube, YouTube brand deals are the way to go. These allow you to make extra money by including a service or product in your videos. You can collaborate with more than one brand to make more money so that you do not only depend on AdSense profits. Unlike the YPP, you'll be able to make money from these deals without stressing about the number of subscribers or watch time you must have.

Rather, focus more on keeping the views you get and making unique content. Once you have both subscribers and views, you'll be well-equipped enough to reach out for YouTube sponsorship. Therefore, you can still find a sponsor without worrying about your channel size. Brand deals are available for every channel size. Every YouTuber has a chance to make money, from the smallest to the largest content creators, and that includes you.

How to Get Sponsored by Brands

Many companies exist that creators can connect with to help them get sponsored by brands. Each of these companies deals with different aspects of the media in order to assist you in getting in contact with the brand that best matches your niche:

- **AIR Media-Tech:** AIR Media-Tech deals with all aspects of advancement for YouTubers. When you open their website, you'll find a step-by-step guide for developing your content career, including offers for creating, distributing, and monetizing content. AIR Media-Tech will help fix your YouTube strikes.

- **Patronage:** It helps companies exchange goods or services for something instead of using money, which will make your experience as a content creator a lot easier.

- **Semaphore:** This company deals with matching creators with brands. Disney, Nintendo, and Audible are a couple of brands that Semaphore has partnered with.

- **Makrwatch:** Brands that can possibly sponsor your content are connected to you through Makrwatch and this happens on a monthly basis. Your free Makrwatch account will give you access to check your sponsorship offers and income.

- **Grapevine Village:** Do you want to create long-term relationships with brands within your niche? Grapevine can assist you in two ways, which are, finding brands to partner with the same niche and keeping you updated on the outcome of the sponsorship. The first thing you'll be required to do before applying is to link your YouTube channel and confirm your identity. Your channel needs to have at least 10,000 subscribers, although micro-influencers are also motivated to register.

- **TapInfluence:** TapInfluence is meant for YouTubers that create fashion, food, lifestyle, and beauty content. You'll have to partner with brands according to your niche, making it simple to match you with a complimentary brand. To enter TapInfluence, the first thing you'll be required to do before applying is to link your YouTube channel and confirm your identity. Next, register for a free account and compile your profile. Then, add the amount you'd like to be paid and some information about the kind of content you make. Petition for working with brands whenever you get an invite from the marketers.

- **Channel Pages:** This is a website used by brands to collaborate with creators. It's mostly used by marketers, who do a lot of research to find channels that match specific campaigns. You might find this exhausting, but a lot of search filters are found on channel pages. Channel pages will make it easier for you to search for something specific within your work using their search filter option. Make sure your channel is listed on this website for brand campaigns so that you don't miss out on gaining more money.

- **Trending Family:** The Trending Family company pairs content creators with brands that encourage family content. For example, a cornflakes ad that includes three siblings and their parents.

- **Spacestation:** It's more based on your make-up, but it's not an ordinary company. The company is more focused on building your career as a content creator through paid sponsorship. Peter McKinnon and Julie Nolke were both assisted by Spacestation to partner with brands like Skillshare and Polar.

- **Aspire:** Are you aware of the creator marketplace? This digital marketplace was built by Aspire to help creators to search for and register for active campaigns.

- **Izea:** Izea gives brands access to get in contact with influencers. You can sign up for free on this platform and create your profile. Just like TapInfluence, Izea is more focused on beauty, lifestyle, and fashion. Izea also has a platform called Shake, where creators can promote their skills and what they have to offer. This market is meant for all creators when you sign up as a seller. From there, people can see what you're offering and purchase your product or services.

YouTube Brand Connect

YouTube has a monetization page called "Brand Connect." This company helps content creators get in contact with brands and their campaigns. The only disadvantage is that YouTube needs to invite you first. However, adjustments might be made in the future, so look out for any updates. As you wait, just make sure you qualify for the program by:

- being a member of the YPP.

- having no evidence of active strikes.

- being over 18 while residing in Canada or the United Kingdom.

Affiliate Marketing

Are you aware that you could make money on YouTube by advertising links? This is what we are referring to as affiliate marketing.

Here is how affiliate marketing works:

- Register for different affiliate programs with various brands and companies.

- Use the customer links provided and share them with your YouTube viewers.

- Earn credit when one of your audience members buys the product using your link.

We recommend that, if you're a beginner, it is best to first sign up for the Amazon Associates Program. Hundreds of links will be available for you to choose from and sharing those links to your content will help you make more income. Additionally, always add links to products that you have reviewed in your videos. For instance, if you review a ring light by showing your audience how it works, direct your viewers to your affiliate link so that they can purchase the product. Affiliate commissions are said to be up to 10% for each product sold on Amazon.

If you would like to learn more about Affiliate Marketing, why not take a look at our book, ***Affiliate Marketing Mastery: The Ultimate Guide to Starting Your Online Business and Earning Passive Income.***

Channel Membership

High-quality content and benefits for your audience are offered to you if you're a channel member. When people watching your videos subscribe to your channel, they get extra benefits such as private live streams, loyalty badges, and high-quality content. As a creator, you have the leverage to decide what works best for your viewers. YouTube Premium membership will help creators make extra money because you'll be able to write down your own amount and display things in your own way. You can charge membership in the range between $0.99 and $100 per month.

Patronage

The Patreon platform permits YouTubers to monetize their content, no matter the niche. Basically, content creators ask their audience to become Patreon users by extending their commitment. This will allow creators to charge their subscribers for high-quality content and make extra money. The amount they charge will depend on the services that they offer; however, creators can charge Patreon users on a monthly basis. Creators are now benefiting more from this than users.

YouTube Live Streams

Those who don't use this feature are probably not aware of how to make money through a YouTube live stream. Well, streaming works the same way as videos; you can add ads to your monetized live streams. Another way to monetize your live streams is through super chats. These are donations ranging from $1 to $500 that your audience can send to you during your live stream. You can only receive Super Chats if:

- you're a comedian or entertainer.

- you constantly host a live stream on YouTube.

- you have a loyal audience that engages in your live streams.

YouTube Shorts Fund

Videos that are up to 60 seconds are called YouTube Shorts. Getting paid for such short videos does not come easy unless they go viral.

YouTube Shorts do not require you to have 4,000 watch hours to get monetized. Qualified short-form creators are paid up to $10,000 per month by the YouTube Shorts Fund. There are several competitors for this amount. Many creators were asked questions about their earnings from YouTube Shorts Funds and the results were as follows:

- **King Probherbs:** A total of 5 million shorts views brought earnings of $300.

- **TN:** A sum of 7 million short views yielded R300.

- **GEVids:** With 130 million shorts views, earnings were $2,300.

This shows that you can monetize short YouTube videos, though the amount is really low.

YouTube Premium

- watching videos with no ads

- no ads when watching YouTube Kids

- downloading videos and opening them later with no internet

- downloading music and listening to it later with no internet

- watching content without logging into the YouTube app

- original YouTube content

Viewers will enjoy these benefits; this works to your advantage as a content creator. While most people enjoy watching uninterrupted videos, content creators find more opportunities to make money on YouTube.

Making Extra Money Using YouTube Premium

How are video creators able to make extra money outside AdSense using YouTube Premium? Well, basically, some of the Premium profits are distributed to video creators. No matter the amount, some of the YouTube Premium profits are shared with creators depending on the amount of watch time they have made through premium subscribers.

For instance, if your channel received a large amount of watch time compared to others, you'll earn more money. For every earning you'll make from the Premium platform, YouTube will take 45% of your creator's earnings.

YouTube AdsThere are different types of ads that are displayed on YouTube videos. Here are some notable examples:

- **Overlay ads:** Ads that play below the video.

- **Display ads:** Ads that are played to the top right of the main video.

- **Skippable video ads:** These ads allow you to select skip after five seconds. Bumper ads: these ads are six seconds long, and don't allow you to skip until the ad is done.

- **Non-skippable video ads:** Ads that can't be skipped.

- **Sponsored cards:** These are ads that correspond to the topic of the video.

How Much Can You Make From Ads?

A new gross sale was announced for July 2020. Creators understand their salary more because their total gross sales per 1,000 views are shown to them. If perhaps you want to follow up on your monthly payment, use that number to calculate your income. It includes the profit you've made, separated from the 45% that is taken by YouTube. Extra profits you've made from YouTube's extra monetization platform, called RPM, are also included. If you want to have a look at your RPM, you'll find them at the bottom of your Analytics page.

The term "CPM" stands for "cost per mile" or more commonly, "cost per thousand," and it refers to how much you earn per 1,000 impressions on your channel. Please note that YouTube would have already charged advertisers before taking 45% off the page. According to Media Shark, the mediocre CPM is known to range between $6 and $8 in the United States. This means that creators will be paid amounts of $6 to $8 per 1,000 ad engagements by advertisers. YouTube will then take 45% of the profit from the $6, $7, or $8, leaving you with $3.30, $3.80, or $4.40 per 1,000 views.

Content That Is Considered Appropriate for All Audiences

To be on the safe side with regard to monetizing your content, make content that is suitable for all audiences. Here are some pointers on what to avoid in your content:

- rough handling of content

- grown-up themes

- foul language

- dehumanization

- hazardous acts

- discrimination

- use of illegal substances

- debates

- staggering videos

- guns or other harmful objects

Merchandise

By now, you probably know your way around making educational videos that your viewers can learn from. In other words, making tutorial videos can be another way for you to make extra money by combining all the videos based on a specific topic to create a course that your subscribers can purchase. Coming up with a most-wanted course can be an advantage to you.

This is an electronic product that will allow you to sell massively. Selling a course for $30 can give you up to $300 each month if only 10 people buy it. Creating a course will not only make you more money, but it will also build your credit score and transform your channel into a business.

However, creating a course is not the only digital product you can sell; there are many more. You can come up with a brand design and start selling it on your platform. For instance, many people love buying T-shirts, hoodies, and hair products. These are some of the things that can help you make more money. If you feel that creating a whole brand to sell can be a bit hectic for you, you can decide to resell, which is a method that many entrepreneurs use to make money.

Below, you'll find a checklist that will guide you through all the steps you should take to monetize your account. This checklist will ensure that you have gone through all the requirements needed for you to have a smooth and successful channel. It will also assist you in making sure that you follow the YouTube guidelines and policies to avoid getting panelized by YouTube or having your channel demonetized.

This chapter explored the various ways through which you can make money on YouTube. We also discussed the requirements that you should meet before you can be able to monetize our channel. In the next chapter, you will get some lessons that were derived from the experiences of fellow YouTubers. Learn from them and enjoy your journey to success.

Checklist

	Gain at least 1,000 subscribers.
	Get 4,000 watch hours in a year.
	Abide by YouTube rules and policies.
	Link your AdSense account to your channel.
	Ensure your channel doesn't have any community guidelines.
	Follow all YouTube monetization policies.
	Have two-step verification set up on your account

Consider and engage some other strategies like affiliate marketing, channel membership, patronage, YouTube shorts, etc.

Chapter 8:

What I Have Learned as a YouTube Content Creator

Alvin Toffler said, "The illiterate of the twenty-first century will not be those who cannot read and write, but those who cannot learn, unlearn, and relearn". This quote is absolutely relevant when it comes to your journey to becoming a money-making pro on YouTube.

As each new day comes, it is accompanied by opportunities to *learn* things that you didn't know on YouTube. There come times when the things that you learned at some point become irrelevant or simply inapplicable because we are in a constantly changing space, especially with regard to technology. If this happens, you should be flexible enough to *unlearn* such things.

Those who are masters of any art have obviously spent a lot of time going through the same processes of learning over and over again. They didn't get tired of learning the same things repeatedly. The same applies to the YouTube business. You should be willing to *relearn* certain things if you are to make it.

In this day and age, the world keeps advancing, and to keep up with it, learning never stops. In the field of content creation, learning from other YouTubers could help you identify mistakes that you can avoid and grow your career as a successful creator. In this chapter, we will share with you some of the lessons that other content creators have learned in their journey as YouTubers and how they've applied them to improve their work.

Have a Clear Why

When you initially start out, you will have the guidance you need if you have a clear motive for starting a YouTube channel. Possessing a compass to guide you will assist you in finding your way to expanding on the platform, regardless of the type of content that you intend to publish or the niche you are in. Know your "whys" in the following areas:

- Why do you want to publish videos on YouTube, not other platforms?

- Why are you confident that you can make it on YouTube, considering the constantly growing fierce competition?

- Why do you think people are going to listen to you? Here, you highlight what makes you unique.

Find Your Niche

Did you know that YouTube receives more than 500 video hours per minute? That is a stunning quantity of information, and YouTube's algorithm is tasked with the enormous burden of determining what is and is not worth presenting to the platform's audience. The objective of YouTube is to keep users on the site for as long as possible. It accomplishes this by linking videos together.

If you produce generic material for a mainstream audience, you are more likely to run into two issues. First, the algorithm won't link to your videos, and second, viewers won't have the incentive to view them. A better approach is to center your channel around a single niche where you can grow into an expert.

The best choice for a niche could be the one that you can discuss with enthusiasm. Imagine producing videos that come out in a more natural manner. You will realize that there are many other content creators who are in the same niche as you. Take a moment to research them and learn from them. Make sure there is a sizable audience for the material that you want to provide because going too specialized on a topic can also backfire.

For example, producing videos on baking, in general, is a good niche that can attract many people who love working with dough and the oven. Now, imagine if you decide to zero in on baking scones only. You are more likely to intensively limit yourself in terms of the audience. Besides, you might end up running out of ideas in the long run.

Learn About Your Target Audience

Making material for a specific audience increases the possibility of attracting more devoted viewers than making videos for everyone. People may quickly search for whatever they want to watch at any moment because of the abundance of information that has been posted on YouTube from across the world. Therefore, you need to have an idea of the words or phrases that your target audience is more likely to use when they search for what to watch on YouTube.

If you ignore that fact, you will continue to go around in circles on YouTube, without growing as you should. If your videos are on electrical home appliances, find out if the audience uses slightly general words like "electronics" or "home appliances." Sometimes, they might specify the exact appliances that they want to hear about so you can include more specific search words like "refrigerator," "stove," or "washing machine" where applicable.

Discover who is watching your material and what additional content they are taking in. You can learn more by reading the comments in other videos. With the help of the platform TubeBuddy, you may find keywords and monitor the behavior of your viewers. Relevant SEO-related information will be released that will assist you in formulating a strategy for increasing engagement from your audience.

This Isn't About You

No matter how much you fall in love with your content and production process, one thing is for sure: It isn't about you. It is more about the audience, who are a very important puzzle to your success as a YouTuber. Many creators overlook the importance of the audience and the knowledge they require. You are the messenger, not the message, even though how you convey your information matters, too.

By disclosing the knowledge you possess, you make it simpler to address queries from your audience and truly provide them with the kind of content they desire. We cannot deny the fact that the audience may become connected to the person that you are but even at that, your aim should be to present yourself in a manner that makes you appealing to the audience. Always keep this in mind—it's more about the audience, not yourself.

Supply Value

You should first consider why someone would want to watch the content ideas that you have before planning and developing them into videos. Before creating their material, new creators often ignore this step and that can be an easy way to brew failure. We will explain why: Knowing why people could be interested in the content that you want to produce helps you to determine if there is an audience for that content. This way, you will avoid making products that no one will ever buy.

Once you are sure that you have an audience, it's crucial to guarantee information-rich material for your audience. Also, ensure that you deliver the quality that matches what YouTube would like its audience to watch. In other words, give your audience solid reasons for streaming your videos, regardless of the type of content you may offer.

Learn From Your Mistakes

Every YouTuber desires to create a video that will come up first in searches by the audience. However, the truth is that this might not be so, especially in the first videos. This might be because you wouldn't have mastered the art of SEO on YouTube. Remember that you can still learn from the "not so good" results—it's a sign of a growth mindset. Do not let previously completed videos discourage you.

Rather use them to identify your areas of improvement and work on making better videos. Be more receptive and extend the scope of your thinking to inspire yourself to produce excellent material.

No One Really Cares About Who You Are

It may be painful for you to learn that in most cases, no one really cares about who you are as a creator. People are more concerned about what you are there to offer. In this generation, people will sell you a falsehood to make you believe they genuinely care about you and the way you live your life. Nobody really knows you, and you're not well-known enough for others to be interested in how you go about your daily business. That is why it takes bloggers longer than other video creators to become popular. Buyers are conducting research to find solutions to their issues. Finding answers to their problems is crucial, despite the fact that amusement may seem to come first.

Most YouTubers who produce vlogs or shows about their lives are well-known or have sizable fan bases. However, they were not always that big and recognized from the beginning. The majority of them kickstarted by developing a brand and actually giving their audience what they needed, which helped them become well-known or gain a sizable following.

Once you've done that, people will naturally start caring more about you and your lunch plans. You will still not get "all-round" care though; the audience has certain things that they are interested in as far as you are concerned.

Serve the Audience

Even though some individuals might not care about you very much, that doesn't imply you're not valuable. Solving your audience's concerns is what matters most. Reminding yourself that you are there to serve your audience is crucial. What purpose does the creation of useless content serve? People use YouTube to find valuable content in addition to getting entertainment. By giving them the information they require, you make it easier for them to believe in you, gain your trust, and make a purchase from you.

Consistency Is Everything

The secret to developing both your YouTube account and your video creation abilities is consistency. A subscriber community should be constantly nurtured and watched. If the videos you upload are the primary means of communication with that audience, you need to make more frequent uploads so that you maintain the connection. Consider it this way—you wouldn't schedule a run with a friend for 8 a.m. every Tuesday and Thursday at the neighborhood park and then fail to show up. Imagine the disappointment! Even worse, you might lose that friend. Your YouTube subscribers are your buddies. You should prove to be consistent so that you gain their confidence.

Learn, Practice, Make More Mistakes, Relearn, Repeat

You don't need camera experience to launch a YouTube channel. All you need is the dedication to do your homework and educate yourself on everything you don't understand. For instance, learn how to:

- do your edits.

- use Final Cut Pro and Adobe Premiere.

- upload your work to YouTube.

The beautiful thing about it all is that YouTube has all the information you could ever want to know about content creation. It will accelerate and ease the learning process. However, keep in mind that the learning process requires a lot of work and is not as easy as it may seem. If you're just starting out, you might not produce high-quality material because you're still learning.

It might seem like nothing is changing, but it shouldn't deter you from pushing on. Give yourself permission to make mistakes so that you can grow from them and develop your abilities. With each new production, you learn something new and also become a better content creator in the process. Your confidence also grows in the process.

Go All-In Right Away

Have you ever heard of the term "Go big or go home"? Well, this is one thing you should consider before launching your YouTube channel. Make sure you have the right equipment if you want to be a successful content creator. It may seem tedious to buy expensive equipment instead of cheap ones before launching your channel but trust the process. It will all make sense once everything is ready. Besides, it is better to invest in long-lasting, high-quality equipment than buy cheap equipment that will last you for a few months.

Please note that doing this is best, but if you can't afford to get the more expensive and possibly durable equipment, you can start with what you have at the moment. This way, you will start the learning process and get more acquainted with the YouTube platform as you improve your production process and equipment.

Build First, Then Advertise

Promoting unfinished content is counterproductive. Instead, concentrate on developing your channel first. Before releasing your recordings for public viewing, you might want to keep them for a few months. Before persuading individuals to view your information, make sure that it is valuable as well.

You'll see that by the time you start promoting your channel, you'll have attracted a sizable following and have a ton of videos available for users to watch. Choosing to stop promoting your channel for a few months will ultimately pay off. You'll begin to be noticed by well-known networks, and you'll also increase your viewers and subscribers.

Before telling people what is happening, work on implementing your ideas. Getting people's attention is useless if they later discover there is nothing on your channel. You want to direct your target audience to a channel that already has videos that can capture their attention and keep them asking for more.

Ask Now, Avoid Later

It's crucial to work on projects with content producers who share your interests. To do this, get in touch with content providers who have comparable followings to you and who produce similar kinds of material. You won't get a response from everyone, but with the ones who do, you'll be able to collaborate and not only build a strong work-related combination but also a friendship. Since you both share similar goals and objectives, you'll both steadily develop your accounts and exchange advice that's in your best interests.

Please note that it is possible to end up in a bad partnership, so you need to be careful when selecting partners for collaboration. Bad partnerships happen when your respective missions and visions diverge, which can cause arguments and misunderstandings, thereby reducing your chances of becoming a successful creator.

If you want to be successful, verify that the people you've chosen to work with share your vision and objectives. This will help to prevent time-related loss and avoidable conflicts. No matter how approachable someone may seem at first, make sure to ask them about their vision and objectives.

There Is No "Main Secret" to Successful Content Creation

There is no secret to becoming a successful creator—your commitment to your work will determine your success. Even though it seems clear, most people tend to avoid doing the actual work when it comes to implementation. A lot of people have brilliant ideas, but only 2%

actually make an effort to move to the implementation stage. You have great content ideas and that's a plus, but acting upon them is what will ignite the dream of becoming a successful content creator to light.

It's a tragic tale, but there are no guarantees in life, and the decisions you make will influence your chances of success. YouTube creators who constantly produce top-notch content adhere to a rigid timetable and have videos planned out weeks in advance. They all have a work ethic that is unmatched by other artists. Their long-term goals took precedence over life's small-minded diversions.

Not everything that you desire to do will come out as planned—that's life and business. Some tasks may even compete for your attention at the same time, so you should learn to prioritize appropriately. That mindset is what you require as a YouTube content creator.

Originality Is Overrated

Everybody imitates someone to a certain extent. Nobody is so creative that they can create all their posts or videos without borrowing ideas from others. As long as the aim is to mimic the style and not the content, you are good to go. At some point, you will be able to merge certain styles and come up with your own. So, until you develop your own style, borrow from others to get things started and gain experience.

The gaming industry was once dominated by prerecorded and manipulated games. Creators shared their highlight games with their audience and chatted about them. The prefabricated videos eventually gave way to live videos from well-known YouTubers. At the time, they claimed to want a new start, but in reality, they were advancing a more advantageous commercial strategy.

Live videos made it easier for creators to upload content every day. That translated into increased daily views and income. Everyone went live a few months later. However, those that benefited the most modified the same live videos and produced them. They achieved the objectives and difficulties established by the audience.

They captured their bizarre reactions. Additionally, they used YouTube as a conduit for live streams on more lucrative websites. Those people personalized a trend that was already popular. And as a result, thousands of new subscribers flocked to them.

By emulating well-known creators, they created their own identities. The blueprint was already there, so they didn't have to start from scratch. Why design a new system when you can modify an existing one to suit your preferences? Compared to the creator, the innovator is much more versatile.

Choose People Over Numbers

While the number of viewers is an important metric on YouTube, focusing only on that can be problematic in the long run. It's not only about the numbers; business involves earning people's trust by looking out for their interests. You develop a positive reputation by doing this. The audience gets devoted to your brand when this is done. Additionally, you receive engagement from devoted viewers.

Do Your Own Thing

The majority of content producers are unaware of this—even if you made edits to other people's videos and add voice-overs, that does not make you the author of the videos you uploaded. This implies that you won't be able to directly monetize your videos. To keep your channel from receiving a copyright strike, you'll need to work with other parties.

When you create and sell your own work, your passion constantly grows. It is easy to lose interest in making content based on someone's work or when they stop making content you are interested in. This may lead to you having nothing to upload on your channel. This is why promoting your work and product is advised because you will have put so much sweat and hours into it. Giving up on your work will not be an option because of the sacrifices you would have made.

Never Underestimate the Power of Marketing

Creating and publishing your videos on YouTube isn't enough. You should engage in robust marketing strategies that will take your business to the next level. You can start with the more traditional ways of marketing, like business cards and putting together a website. Currently, there are various digital methods for getting your videos out there to the people who are more likely to find them interesting.

Social media platforms such as LinkedIn, Facebook, and X will certainly boost the visibility of your content. You can even create blogs and embed links to your videos. This Is effective because there are greater chances that the people who read through your blogs might be interested in the videos as well.

Don't Just Accept Everything That Comes Your Way

As an upcoming content creator on YouTube, you will be hungry for growth and that's normal. As time progresses, you might get many offers for collaborations and possible support. The urge to accept virtually everything will also be huge but you need to be careful. Know what you want and evaluate offers before accepting any of them. You don't want to accept offers that will, for example, end up making you someone's puppet while leaving your own goals.

You might also debate whether to be a full-time YouTuber or not. Also, weigh your options carefully. If you are not yet earning much from YouTube, you should keep your other job so that you don't lose out on your sole source of income. As your YouTube business grows, there is no harm in considering your decisions accordingly, though there's still no need to rush.

Solve Problems

Videos that solve cheating problems for your audience will yield constant engagement from the audience. The engagement is also more likely to be long-term. While viral videos and certain trends are generally good because they will give you spikes in likes, comments, and shares, engagement is usually short-lived. YouTube is currently investing in YouTube Shorts and there is no harm in trying them. However, don't completely leave the videos that you make to solve the problem of your viewers.

Take Good Care of Yourself

Remember, without you, your business is not there. Therefore, you need to take care of yourself so that you can be available to deliver amazing content to your audience. Eat healthily and reduce indulgence in foods that have too many refined sugars and unhealthy fats. Get some time to take care of your physical health by exercising and getting medical attention when you are not feeling well. You also need good sleep—about eight hours of sleep on average is good enough. Also, take care of your mental health using methods such as meditation. It's also fine to take a break when you feel that you are not ready to work. You deserve it; you work so hard after all.

There Is No Best Time to Start

It is common for people to assume that there is a perfect time during which they can launch their YouTube channels. However, the truth of the matter is that there isn't such a time. Usually, it is fear and anxiety that makes you think that there is a best time for recording and possibly uploading your videos yet even the most experienced YouTubers will tell you that even now, they never feel prepared.

Getting Comfortable With the Camera Is Not Easy

Being a YouTuber means that you will be working with the camera a lot. However, if you are not an actor who loves the camera, it is more likely that you are going to have a hard time. Talking to an audience who can blink and affirm what you're saying feels a lot better than talking to the camera. Take some time to record videos of yourself as many times as you can so that you can get used to talking in front of the lens.

Practice Is an Essential Part of the Game

The chances that your first project will be so good are very slim. You will probably produce something that you might not be so proud of, compared to the subsequent ones. It is a continued practice that makes things work out better as time progresses. So, there is no point in giving up when things don't seem to go well at first. Rather, soldier on and you will be glad you did!

Work on Getting Acquainted With the Process

You should find ways to befriend the process of making videos so that it doesn't get as scary as it might be when you start. As we mentioned earlier, it is normal for you to be nervous when you are in front of the camera. Even established public speakers do experience the same nerves, especially when they know that what they are saying is being recorded. Here is a tip that can help you to relax—remind yourself of two things:

- that you can always retake if you fumble.

- that both the camera and the channel are yours, and besides, it's not live.

Better Get Done Than Wait for a Perfect Version

Creating videos requires you to be forgiving and kind to yourself. You are more likely to make many mistakes, and this can be quite frustrating at times. Experience will teach you that reaching that "perfect" state when making videos could be far from reality for quite a long time, if not for the rest of your career as a YouTuber. After all, those pauses, gasps, and conversational touches that you might see as imperfections might be what the audience identifies with for your uniqueness. You will also appear more real. Therefore, publish what you have and go back to making even more videos.

Checklist

The ideas that are outlined in this chapter can be divided into three categories, which are, before, during, and after production. We have created one table with the categories clearly laid out. Do what you feel is relevant and place a tick under the "yes" column.

Here is a checklist for the implementation of important tips for YouTubers.

Before production • There is no best time to start. • Take good care of yourself. • Come up with content ideas that solve people's problems. • Learn from other YouTubers. • Find your niche. • Have good reasons why you are starting your YouTube channel.	
During production • Better get done and publish than wait for the perfect version. • Work on getting acquainted with the production process. • Get comfortable with the camera. • Be authentic and find your own voice. • Focus on the quality more than luring subscribers. • Put in your best right from the start. • Focus on delivering valuable content.	

After production
- Continue to practice.
- Don't just accept everything that comes your way but weigh options wisely.
- Engage in intensive marketing.
- Keep trying and find what works for you.
- Engage in effective and authentic collaboration with other YouTubers.
- Embrace consistency in production schedules.
- Learn from your mistakes.

Learning from the experiences of other YouTubers is a great way to learn relevant tips. This chapter provided you with a wealth of information that helps you to start your YouTube channel with knowledge and more confidence. There is nothing to wait for, it's time to get the tips for useful implementation.

Conclusion

Publishing videos on YouTube begins by finding a niche that matches the type of content that you want to deliver. There are many niches that are available, and they include cooking, beauty, and gaming, just to mention a few. You need to do quality research for you to determine a suitable niche. Other factors that you should consider when finding a niche are:

- going for a niche that is within a niche.

- identifying a niche that meets the needs of the audience that you are targeting.

- selecting a niche that has less competition.

The next step that we highlighted in this book was setting up and managing your channel. We outlined all the steps that you need for you to set up your channel. To start making videos to add to your channel, you should have a camera, external microphone, lighting equipment, editing software, as well as a tripod or a gimbal stabilizer. As you start off, you can even use a phone with a good camera for taking your videos, so there is nothing that can stop you.

As time progresses, you should focus more on improving the quality of your video content. Better quality should be seen from the ideas, video shooting, audible sound, and relatable visuals. Generally, a good content strategy has four main components, which are:

- **Brand focus**, which is what you represent.

- **User experience**, which describes how your content addresses the concerns of the audience.

- **Content distribution**, which focuses on how your content will be distributed for the audience to find it.

- **Content creation**, which is the glue between the first three components.

Once you are able to deliver quality content, your focus should be on growing your subscriber base. Strategies that you can use in getting this done include using power playlists, publishing more frequently, optimizing your videos, and using brand watermarks. You also need to understand how to get the YouTube algorithm to your side. One of the ways you can do that is by incorporating relevant keywords in your titles and video descriptions. This will help your videos to pop up when the YouTube audience uses the search engine to look for videos that answer their search queries.

Growing your subscribers on YouTube is one thing, and enhancing audience engagement is another thing. YouTube promotes videos that have greater audience engagement because it assumes that they provide content that is loved by people and has good quality.

Therefore, we recommend that you use YouTube Analytics to assess your current audience engagement status so that you can know how best you can boost yourself in this area. Some of the ideas that you can consider in boosting audience engagement on YouTube include creating custom thumbnails, interacting with the viewers, using calls-to-action, and collaborating with other YouTubers.

Like any other venture, YouTube requires that you adopt the right mindset that is supportive of success. Carol Dwek presents the fact that there are basically two types of mindsets, which are: growth and fixed. The growth mindset is flexible to change while the fixed one is not. As a YouTuber, you are recommended to create and nurture a growth mindset progressively. It's something that you can work on every day. Practices such as reading, physical exercise, and meditation are supportive of a growth mindset.

After all is said and done, you still need to make some money from your channel. Please note that you can only monetize your channel if you reach a certain number of subscribers. Also, you should be part of the YPP. There are various ways through which you can make money on YouTube, and these include affiliate marketing, getting sponsorship, and YouTube BrandConnect.

The book ends by outlining tips that assist you to make your journey as a YouTube content creator even more successful. These include but are not limited to the encouragement to:

- learning from your mistakes.

- practicing over and over again.

- focusing on serving the audience.

- taking care of yourself so that you avoid burnout.

It is our sincere desire that this book guides you to achieving your dream of becoming a successful YouTube content creator who makes money on the platform. Happy money-making escapade!

Thank you!

Before you go, we just wanted to say thank you for purchasing our book. You could have picked from dozens of other books on the same topic but you took a chance and chose this one. So, a HUGE thanks to you for getting this book and for reading all the way to the end.

Now, we wanted to ask you for a small favor. COULD YOU PLEASE

CONSIDER POSTING A REVIEW ON THE PLATFORM? (Reviews are one of the easiest ways to support the work of independent authors.)

This feedback will help us continue to write the type of books that will help you get the results you want.

So if you enjoyed it, please let us know here: http://amazon.com/review/create-review/asin=B0C8LWYPP7!

We wish you much Success on your Journey!

Printed in Dunstable, United Kingdom

64405257R00107